0/96

Footloose on the
Santa Fe Trail

Footloose on the Santa Fe Trail

by Stephen May

University Press of Colorado

Copyright © 1993 by the University Press of Colorado

Published by the University Press of Colorado
P.O. Box 849
Niwot, Colorado 80544

The University Press of Colorado is a cooperative publishing enterprise supported, in part, by Adams State College, Colorado State University, Fort Lewis College, Mesa State College, Metropolitan State College of Denver, University of Colorado, University of Northern Colorado, University of Southern Colorado, and Western State College of Colorado.

Library of Congress Cataloging-in-Publication Data

May, Stephen.
  Footloose on the Santa Fe trail / by Stephen May.
    p.
  ISBN 0-87081-294-7 (alk. paper). — ISBN 0-87081-295-5 (pbk.: alk. paper)
  1. Santa Fe Trail — History. I. Title.
  F786.M47 1993
  979 — dc20   93-19431
                                                                   CIP

The paper used in this publication meets the minimum requirements of the American National Standard for Information Sciences — Permanence of Paper for Printed Library Materials. ANSI Z39.48–1984

∞

10 9 8 7 6 5 4 3 2 1

The Open Road. The great home of the soul is the open road. Not heaven, not paradise. Not "above." Not even "within." The soul is neither "above" nor "within." It is a wayfarer down the open road.

— D. H. LAWRENCE

Other Books by Stephen May

Pilgrimage: A Journey Through Colorado's History and Culture
Fire From the Skies
A Land Observed: The West of the American Painter

Contents

Preface

This is a story of a journey into and through the heart of the American West. I took the trip for two reasons: the desire to see the terrain, the people, and the culture of the area, and at the same time to imagine what this historic region was like more than 150 years ago.

To accomplish the latter, I chose to focus on the events of one year — 1846 — and part of another — 1847 — that comprised a significant if not portentous period in the development of the West. Never in the settling of the West had there been a year when so much military, literary, artistic, and cultural activity occurred in such a compact region. In short, it was a time when all the dynamic elements of the human drama reached a brief apogee.

I thought it might be interesting to compare and contrast my own modern journey with the exploits and travels of people who lived in that other era. I have always been an avid walker, so the idea of a looping trek along the Santa Fe Trail and around the Sangre de Cristos, traveling the routes of the nineteenth century and sleeping under the simple stars, seemed not only tantalizing but within my reach. I laid out the specific historical routes on a map and soon realized that with a good walk I could cover the experiences of some of the most dramatic personalities of the age and yet still encounter a modern view of southern Colorado and northern New Mexico.

What resulted is this account of my own adventures in the western heartland and those of Francis Parkman, Henry Chatillon, Susan and Samuel Magoffin, Ceran St. Vrain, Stephen Kearny, Charles and William Bent, Lewis Garrard, and George Frederick Ruxton. There was a surprise addition, however. A chance encounter with a stranger on a Colorado back road led me to discover another lesser-known traveler from that year. Without this stroke of good fortune, I probably would not have written this book.

When I finished, I realized that I had entered the lives of three writer-adventurers, a merchant's wife, an army commander, a carpenter, and a territorial governor. Essentially, this is the story of how these peoples' lives became intertwined by the events of 1846–1847. It should be noted that in dramatizing these historical figures' lives I have in some episodes fictionalized their actions, thoughts, and feelings. Additionally, to avoid impeding the flow of the narrative, I have often not used formal citations. Readers can find these sources in the References section in the back of this book.

I would like to thank the Colorado Historical Society and the New Mexico Historical Society for their help in the preparation of this book. Special thanks go to George (Golden Hawk) Bennett, who provided valuable commentary on the fur trade sections.

This book is aimed primarily at young people who live in the West, who are active, mobile, and ambitious, and who are exceptionally curious about and rightfully proud of their western heritage. To them, and to my brother, Brian, who can't get enough of western spaces, this book is respectfully dedicated.

Footloose on the
Santa Fe Trail

❧

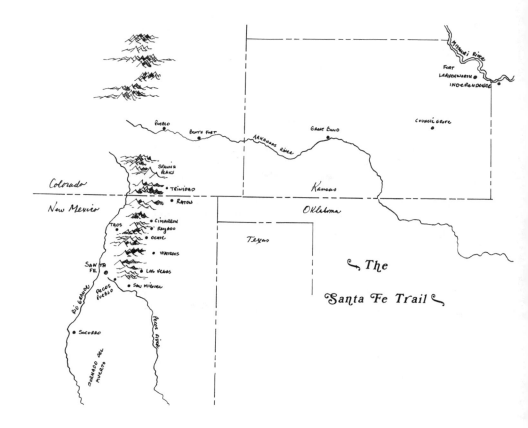

The
Santa Fe Trail

Part One
Caravans

1. Citadel on the Prairie

The second thing people want to know is what type of shoes I wear while walking long distances. I tell them straight out. I wear a pair of Merrell walkers, and an extra pair is tucked away in my pack for alternate use. I don't favor heavy hiking boots. They are much too hot and cumbersome, and by the end of the day my feet feel like dead weights dangling from my kneecaps. Give me a pair of sturdy, lightweight walking shoes any day.

This brings me to the first thing people are curious about. This question often requires a more complex answer, and sometimes even that response is colored by how I feel and how tired my legs are that day. People want to know why I walk the distances I do. Particularly they are interested in this little jaunt from Colorado to New Mexico and back. Actually, I was reflecting on this very subject in my friend Paul's cabin in the mountains west of Pueblo the evening before the day I was to leave.

It was about eight o'clock and the wind had died to a murmur. The sun outlined the threadbare edges of the curtain at the window. In the silence of the forest outside, a lone magpie squawked its grievances to an indifferent world. Paul's place was roomy; several muscular, torn armchairs surrounded a rock fireplace. Newspapers and magazines littered the end tables. Several prints by Chagall and Magritte hung on the rough pine walls — oddities, really, in this jumbled bracken of rustic fixtures and odds and ends. Paul sat across from me smoking a pipe. He blew several ragged smoke rings into the air, stroked his chin with the pipe stem, and stared at me. The smoke smelled of oranges and pine tar.

"So tell me again why you're going," he said presently.

"Several reasons." I turned in my chair. "For one, I'm bored. I need to move again. For another, I need to experience a land and people again. There are several ideas whirling in my head that are still obscure. I hope they'll become clearer as I start walking. They usually do."

I paused. "I could ask you why you want to stay home."

He smiled. "Yes, you could. I have my job, of course. Sarah's due home from Denver this week and I'd like to be here when she arrives. The pipes are corroding under the floor where you sit. In two days I'm due at the county commissioner's office to argue a zoning violation. I think Jeff's got the chicken pox. And so on and so on."

"The web of life?"

"Sounds like it, doesn't it?"

Paul knocked the ashes from his pipe. Getting up, he circled the room, peered out the window, and finally returned to his chair. He sat on its edge, his hands cupping the warm bowl of his pipe. It was near dark, and the last feeble rays of sun filtered through the curtains and fell upon Paul's bemused face, softening his features and lighting the ginger hairs of his two-day-old beard.

"I envy you," he said.

"Why don't you come with me?"

"You know I can't."

"For part of the trip?" I urged.

He nibbled at the pipe stem, smothering a belch. "Which part?"

"Let's say the return part. When I get back to Colorado. I can call you and set it up well in advance. Then your agenda might be a little clearer."

"Three or four days?" he asked sheepishly.

"The most scenic part of the trip."

"O.K. Where are you going to start?"

"I'd thought of starting at Bent's Fort. It's relatively close and I wanted a historical pivot from which to begin. Besides, it has some historical and cultural associations that are important to me."

"Want me to drive you there?"

"I knew you wouldn't mind."

"I wouldn't mind," he snarled affectionately. "Want some coffee?"

"Yes."

Paul owns four cars. Three are usually disabled and lined up in the driveway like recalcitrant dogs waiting for their baths. But the fourth is a spitfire: a sleek red '74 Porsche that is emperor of the road. The Porsche had just enough room for us and my gear. It was a late June morning, and as we pushed along the highway between Pueblo and Bent's Fort the sun was well up in the sky and beginning to warm and sting.

Dry fields stretched toward oases of cottonwoods on either side of the road. It had not rained in five days. The sky looked soiled and impotent. The heat rose, trembling in soft waves over the arid grass. Clouds that would never rain began to gather and loiter over the distant barns and creeks, their undersides the color of gruel.

The flaming air punished our faces, but the Porsche cut right through it. The sun bolted through a corner of the window, flashing in our eyes and turning the seats as hot as glowing coals. The radio cranked out a song about how love resembled a flat tire. I never quite got the connection, even though the spirited group repeated the words close to fifteen times. The world rushed by, hoarse singing, guitars, deflated tires, drums, the suck of wheels on pavement accompanying our passage down the road. Unconsciously I put my foot on the glove compartment and added my own rhythm. Paul peered over his sunglasses at me. Chastised, I lowered my foot and stared out the window.

Bent's Fort stands alone on the prairie like a lost child looking in all directions for its parents. We arrived about noon. Having parked the car in an isolated spot, we entered the fort's gates and circled the quadrangle for a full half-hour. Tourists and pilgrims, dressed in T-shirts and toting cameras, wandered about in the dusty courtyard. Babies wailed and boys chased their sisters along the creaking planks adjoining the hot adobe walls. In one corner, a blacksmith pounded a red-hot horseshoe against an anvil; in another, a burly carpenter repaired a broken Conestoga wheel; in yet another, a matronly, no-nonsense woman of the temperance school stirred a boiling cauldron of stuff truly fit for someone else: pioneers, I guessed.

We continued to stroll and talk, I drinking in the haunting separation of yesterday and today. There is no history. Truly, the study of history is simply the examination of profound moments in extraordinary lives. We walked toward one of the rooms, and a Pomeranian on a leash pissed on a post, as if to tell Paul and me what it thought of sacred places. Its master whistled a tune and looked the other way.

We crossed the cool shadows of the low porch and entered one of the commander's rooms. As we came in, we passed a man wearing a bright T-shirt that warned, "Life's a bitch. Then you die." I looked quickly at Paul, who shook his head. The room smelled of cold mud, straw, and ancient rivers. In front of us a table was carefully decked out in a pressed lace tablecloth, tarnished candelabra, and nineteenth-century flatware. Crystal salt and pepper shakers stood proudly in the center of the table. For a moment I did not speak or move. Finally I went up to one of the chairs and placed my hands on its back.

"Holt," I murmured.

"Huh?" said Paul.

I patted the back of the chair. "Holt sat here. Parkman there. No, there." I moved to another chair. "Shaw sat here. Chatillon there, and Deslauriers there."

Paul regarded me with confusion from across the table.

I looked up and smiled. "Never mind. I was just musing about a summer day a century and a half ago. Or perhaps it was yesterday, or last week."

In early May 1846, twenty-three-year-old Francis Parkman, fresh from St. Louis and the East "on a tour of curiosity and amusement to the Rocky Mountains," as he described it, rode into Independence, Missouri. It was his first time in this part of the West, having come from Boston and Harvard, and what he saw filled his mind with new images and colors: storehouses, shacks, saloons, wagons, horses milling around at every corner; men from Vermont, Ohio, New York, and Pennsylvania spilling out from the public houses into the streets; and a lone young girl riding in her Sunday homespun, holding a parasol over her head.

As this was the beginning of both the Oregon and Santa Fe trails, the knots of men, women, and children were bivouacking and planning their different routes. The trail to Oregon moved west from Independence to Westport, crossed the Kansas River, and swept northward onto the prairies of Kansas and Nebraska. Following the

Platte River partway to Fort Laramie, it cut through South Pass in Wyoming and headed for the high country of eastern Oregon. Santa Fe traders, too, gathered in Independence, playing cards, guzzling whiskey, and tallying cargo, impatient for their journey across the plains to the Mexican province called New Mexico. One section of the Santa Fe Trail followed the Arkansas River to Bent's Fort, headed south to Raton Pass, and then traced the curve of the Sangre de Cristo mountains to Santa Fe. The other section headed nearly due southwest through what is now Oklahoma.

As it turned out, Francis Parkman would take both the Oregon and Santa Fe trails. He would ride the prairies north to Fort Laramie, sojourn in a Sioux village, head south along Colorado's Front Range, turn east at Pueblo, and then head for Bent's Fort and Missouri. This trianglular journey not only gave him a glimpse of emigration, topography, and commerce, but also put him in an important section of the country during a crucial time for traveling Americans. It was crucial in two respects: the great tide of western expansion was pouring onto the Oregon Trail that season, and the war with Mexico was imminent on the southern horizon. One major reason for the war was America's wish to acquire land held by Mexico, so that Manifest Destiny could be achieved. While Parkman was in Independence counting Baltimore drunkards, Col. Stephen Kearny was close by, awaiting orders to move his Army of the West southwest to Santa Fe. In Texas alarm led to action, and Gen. Zachary Taylor repulsed a Mexican army near the Gulf. Meanwhile, Mexicans were attacking California by sea. If Parkman was not directly affected by the swirl of events that summer, his contemporaries traveling in other parts of the region certainly were, and we shall see how they fared as they arrived in the West later that season.

A few more words about Parkman before we turn him loose on the trail bound for the Rockies. He was born to influential and respectable Boston parents, grew up reading about the frontier in works by Washington Irving and James Fenimore Cooper, became a deadeye with a rifle, graduated from Harvard with a law degree in 1844, and was in most cases an outright snob. But he was a snob with a sharp eye, and this he used to a distinct advantage in traveling west.

At first there were four in Parkman's party. Parkman was invariably clad in a red flannel shirt and moccasins, as was his Boston cousin Quincy Adams Shaw. The muleteer, called Deslauriers, was a rascally French Canadian who was impervious to the dangers of the prairie. Their guide was thirty-year-old Henry Chatillon, a veteran scout and frontiersman who was to spend most of his life in the Rocky Mountain region. Generous, illiterate, a sharpshooter with a rifle, and deadly with a tomahawk, Chatillon was the kingpin in Parkman's caravan. The scout had taken an Indian bride, Bear Robe, who was the daughter of Bull Bear, chief of the Oglalas, and on the strength of this association Parkman was allowed the nearly complete run of a Sioux village later in the expedition. Chatillon had been hired for Parkman by P. Chouteau, Jr., and Company, whose outposts Chatillon had stocked with buffalo. He was a gentleman, a superb hunter, a trusted friend, a man for all seasons and situations on the great prairies. In that year of 1846 he may well have been the finest all-round scout and hunter in the West. He was the real Natty Bumppo, except that Chatillon was St. Louis French. The French were often to play key roles in the winning of the West.

On May 10, 1846, the four ferried across the Kansas River. The flowers danced on the prairies, lilacs crowded the shoreline, bees buzzed in the wet shadows of the maples, and farther on the green of the plains' grasses was dappled in cloud shadow and rich light. The sun shone, a feeble warm sun — tender as an angel's kiss compared to the monster's embrace the group would encounter out on the prairie.

In a day they reached Fort Leavenworth, where they camped. Kearny's dragoons loafed in the shade, cleaned their rifles, and idly prepared for their march on Santa Fe. After visiting a Kickapoo village nearby, Parkman met Colonel Kearny and shared a bottle of fine claret with him and a British captain named Chandler. The captain was in a frothy mood. He spoke of steeplechases and buffalo hunts: he was always talking nonsense. Parkman knew him from Westport in the days previous. Romaine, Chandler's sidekick, also lounged with them, guzzling the last of the wine. Parkman and Chandler agreed to join forces for the journey (at least partway, as it turned out). Kearny drained his glass of claret; Parkman followed;

they joked. From now on it was brackish water, sand flies, rattle-snakes, dust, and Sioux.

On May thirteenth the enlarged group turned northwest onto the prairie — Parkman, Shaw, Deslauriers, Chatillon, and the English party composed of Chandler, his brother Jack, Romaine, and two hunters. The plain undulated ahead of them, bare except for the ravines of cottonwoods that relieved the lime green of the grass. In the mornings the sun rose in an empty sky and pulsed in the still air. In the afternoons the sky clouded over, the wind eddied, and thunderstorms thrashed down on their march. When he was in Missouri, Parkman had observed that "the clouds in this region are afflicted with an incontinence of water," but as the group moved out onto the prairies of Kansas, the clouds became sparser and drier. The travelers were lucky at times to get a sprinkle on their parched lips. Incontinence of water indeed.

They headed north toward the Little Blue River, fording streams whose mud bogged down the wagon wheels. At every crossing Deslauriers jumped down and ran off a string of the French oath "Sacre———!" They unloaded the wagons and pressed on. Ahead of them, emigrant wagons creaked up the rutted trail that led to the Platte River.

On the twenty-fourth, Parkman and company camped near one of the emigrant parties. Captain Chandler saddled his horse and rode over to greet them. He chatted with the group's leader, a man named Kearsley. Later the captain told Parkman that the women were "damned ugly." Kearsley felt impelled to ride back to Parkman's camp and complain to the group that the emigrants were already beginning to haggle among themselves. Parkman was glad he was with a small group of men, even though Chandler got on his nerves.

Pushing on, Parkman's group filed past grim reminders of those who had preceded them on the strenuous trail march. Crude, wooden crosses had been stuck into the sand by the side of the trail. Wolf tracks appeared around the shallow graves, just next to the steady trail of horse, mule, and ox prints. Someone had ripped a plank from a wagon, burned onto it the rough letters "Mary Ellis, died, May 7th, 1845, aged two months," and wedged it into a small hill. As the travelers climbed toward the Platte, the crosses and wolf tracks increased.

They were now north of the Little Blue River, with the Platte valley in view. Emigrant parties crowded the trail ahead of and behind them. Parkman and the English soon overtook a party of Missourians who were plodding along at a steady tortoise's pace. As Parkman and Shaw passed their wagon, several children poked their grimy faces through the opening and stared at the mounted interlopers. The women dropped their knitting. One of the men called out to them, "How are ye boys? Are ye for Oregon or California?"

Parkman's group pressed on past the struggling oxen. They did not speak. None of your damned business, thought Parkman.

This specific prejudice against the advancing emigrants shaped Parkman's thinking and actions throughout the entire trek. He knew his white brothers. He had seen Missourians, Kentuckians, and New Englanders in St. Louis and Independence. He saw their drunken stupidity, oafish inaction, and corrosive greed. Forget this noble enterprise they were now engaged in. Forget that. He knew them better. I know my foolish white brothers, he said to himself; show me mountain men, buffalo, Indians, strangeness.

He did not have to wait long to meet Indians, as they soon entered the heart of Pawnee country.

Washington Irving, one of Parkman's literary idols, had enjoyed peaceful dealings with Indians, partly because Irving's adventures in Oklahoma in 1832 (chronicled in his *Tour on the Prairies*) took place when the southern Pawnees and Osages were relatively peaceful and unaffected by white emigration. In 1846, however, the Pawnees in Nebraska were seeing streams of wagon trains crossing their lands. The Pawnees were known for stealing weapons and horses, but they could also kill as violently as their neighbors the Sioux. Regarding the Sioux, Parkman was lucky this year. They were not yet hostile toward whites, and in their country, due west, they carried on their rituals much as they had for centuries.

These rituals Parkman wanted to see; the prospect made his blood race. He stood in awe of Indians, be they Pawnees, Sioux, Snakes, or Arapahos, hypnotized by what he imagined to be their nakedness and blood lust. He admired and feared them because they didn't follow his laws. If they could understand him, he thought, he would say, "I'm Francis Parkman from Boston and Harvard," and they would snarl and shake their knives. That was the reaction he wanted, something that slapped the heart and made it listen. That was communication: not some fellow white traveler calmly asking him in Missouri English where the hell he was going.

When they reached the Platte, the land ahead swelled and simmered in the dull-gray heat haze. The river snaked through the rolling sand hills covered with knee-high prairie grasses. Gorges and ravines sliced through the hills, sweeping down in dark scars into the river bank. A few trees dotted the hillsides, but mainly they followed the course of the river. The Platte was half a mile wide and two feet deep. The hot sun beat on the surface of the water, illuminating the subtle currents and the mud banks toward the edges where the buffalo came down at night to drink and wallow.

The party usually camped by the river. One morning Parkman and Chatillon looked up to see a Pawnee hunting party approaching. The two stood silently as thirty or so braves filed by within two hundred yards of them. Bearing bows and arrows, and naked except for breechcloths, they led ponies laden with dried meat. The braves eyed Parkman, Chatillon, and the others. Parkman steadied his nerves, walked over to the group, and handed the bony chief some tobacco. Garbed in an old, shaggy buffalo robe, the chief snatched the tobacco in his grimy hand and smiled. It wasn't a smile, really: more a brief curl of the lip. Parkman thought this a promise of adventures to come.

Continuing to follow the Platte, Parkman, Shaw, Chatillon, and Deslauriers, together with Chandler and company, looked for signs of buffalo. In the first week of June, bludgeoned by the heat and bitten by sand flies, they found a large herd near the river. Circling the herd, they spurred their horses down the sloping ravine where several of the buffalo had gathered. Shaw went on a wild ride into a cloud of dust. Pontiac, Parkman's horse, bolted forward in pursuit of a bull. Pontiac was not used to these prairie skirmishes and would not press close to the shoulder of the running bull. Parkman fired from a distance and hit the bull in the rear. Unaffected, the bison charged up a hill and disappeared into another ravine. Parkman returned for another assault.

Meanwhile, the herd had scattered. Chatillon and Shaw were nowhere to be seen. Parkman reloaded his pistols and headed west. His next pursuit carried him still farther from his companions. Suddenly each hill, ravine, and patch of sky looked the same. The buffalo had gone; he was sweating and exhausted — and lost. Embarrassed and confused, but still keeping his head about him, he followed some old buffalo paths to a point just west of camp. He plodded on eight more miles before seeing Chatillon and Shaw advancing over a hill. The prairie had at last greeted the cool Boston sharpshooter.

By the second week of June they reached the South Fork of the Platte, about 150 miles short of their objective, Fort Laramie. With the splitting of the Platte came the breakup of the group. Parkman and his group wanted to hasten the journey, while Captain Chandler and his party wished to slow down. Parkman and Chatillon thought Chandler was trying to anger and annoy the Americans, and since they wished to press on to Fort Laramie with utmost speed, they could not tolerate the captain's sloth. Upon hearing of Parkman's intent to part company, Chandler gruffly remarked, "A very extraordinary proceeding, gentlemen!"

Before sunrise the next day, Parkman and the others bundled up the tents, harnessed the horses, and left the English contingent wrapped in their plaids on a nearby hill.

The original four — Parkman, Shaw, Chatillon, and Deslauriers — plugged along to Fort Laramie, following the Platte and observing Scott's Bluff and Chimney Rock, landmarks that heralded the temporary end of the trail.

2. Bostonian in Buckskin

Paul and I had walked outside so that he could smoke his pipe. The sun had continued its fierce run in the sky, but now a skimpy maverick cloud temporarily threw a pathetic shadow over the quadrangle. The crowds had thinned since noon. The spunky Pomeranian and its master had melted into the group over by the blacksmith shop. The sounds of hammering and sawing still rose spasmodically from the darkness under the heavy turret in the corner. The American flag hung limply above the gates and rampart ahead of us.

We found a crude pine bench in the shade and sat down. Fumbling for his tobacco pouches, Paul finally selected a crumpled one, gingerly opened the top, stuffed his fingers into the contents, and filled the bowl of his pipe. He caressed the top of the bowl with several strokes of his index finger. He struck a match on the bench and brought it quickly to the bowl; a brief puff of smoke exploded, rose, and drifted out into the quad. He sucked madly on the stem, the amber juice gurgling in the little hole and trickling into the corner of his mouth.

Having completed this ritual, Paul gripped the pipe in his teeth, leaned back against the adobe wall, and laced his fingers over one knee. He squinted at the rampart and the bright sky above. "I suppose Parkman found his Sioux village," he said.

I too leaned against the wall and stared out over the quad, sensing a feeble current of air brushing like a kitten against my arms and face.

"Yes," I said, "he found it — in a roundabout way, as I recall. A couple of things to keep in mind, though. Shaw and Deslauriers were basically adventurers, and after they got to Fort Laramie they were content to let fate take them where it wanted. Parkman, of course, had come over a thousand miles to see an Indian village, and by God he was going to see one. But there were circumstances he had not counted on. For one, Henry Chatillon's wife, Bear Robe, was ill and dying. Henry dropped what he was doing and headed into the wilderness with Shaw to find her. But now we really *are* getting ahead of ourselves."

Established by the American Fur Company, Fort Laramie stood two-thirds of the way between Independence and South Pass, at the confluence of the Platte and Laramie Creek. In 1846 the fort was particularly brimming with emigration spirit. The parties pulled in, camped in clusters, and turned their horses, cattle, and oxen loose in the high grass on the banks of the river. The emigrant trains competed for space with a multitude of Oglala and Brulé Sioux tepees surrounding the fort. Chiefs and young warriors demanded feasts from the transient parties, also requesting a toll of biscuits, bacon, or tobacco. Sitting in small circles between the Oregon-bound wagons, the Indian men gulped coffee, wolfed food, smoked Virginia tobacco in their long pipes, glowered menacingly, and waited for the next wagon train to arrive. Half-naked pioneer children, freed from the wagons, cavorted in the cold shallows of Laramie Creek. That June, great hunters and mountain men such as Pierre Louis Vasquez were bunking here too. Times were good at the fort. They wouldn't last.

Secure within the fort's fifteen-foot-high walls and secluded in the darkness of their rooms, Parkman and Shaw threw buffalo rugs on the floor, stripped their tattered clothing from their backs, and had their first shave in weeks. Barely had they gotten settled when several Indian men filed into their room, shook their hands in greeting, and demanded they smoke the pipe. These men were the fathers, brothers, and other relatives of the women at the fort, and this was a way of making known the women's availability. They smoked and grunted on Parkman's rugs. The Indians then rose and began shaking and fondling the white men's compasses, telescopes, and trinkets. Parkman stood back watching as they shook the objects.

It was mid-June, in midyear, in midcentury, in an America in midstream, and small personal dramas like Parkman's were being played out within a larger pageant of cavalry, infantry, and artillery under the command of a brash colonel hoping to extend American territory from Bent's Fort to the Pacific Ocean. But if Stephen

Kearny's objectives were relatively clear that summer, Parkman's were as hazy as bogies shimmering in a prairie mirage.

Dysentery felled him. For hours Parkman would lie prone on his rug, unable to ride or even to read his Byron. This setback came at a time when the party was planning its next move: a journey out of Fort Laramie to witness a Sioux expedition against the Snakes. Here was his chance. A week at the fort dining on dog meat (a common entree of the era), listening to Pierre Louis Vasquez, and watching the emigrant trains arrive and leave was quite enough. If Parkman was going to be an observer of Indian life, he was going to have to do it on their trails, in their tepees.

Adding to his frustration was the news of the illness of Chatillon's wife, which had prevented the group from attending a major Sioux rendezvous at La Bonté Creek. Parkman loved Chatillon by this time, and he soon agreed to put aside any other plans and accompany the scout to find his wife's village.

Parkman never made it. As he lay, too weak to ride further, near the Chugwater River fifty miles southwest of Laramie, Chatillon and Shaw headed into the high country. Parkman eventually turned back temporarily to Fort Laramie.

While Chatillon and Shaw hurried toward her, Bear Robe lay speechless and immobile in her lodge near the Chugwater. She stared and waited for Henry, life ebbing from her. How she loved him now; how she waited for his confident voice and gentle hand to lift her soul; how she knew now that only briefly would she feel his touch.

He arrived that night; she rallied; they talked till morning. After sunrise, Chatillon and Shaw lifted her onto a travois and, accompanied by men and women from the village, set out for help. Chatillon and Shaw, mounted, led the way. Only two miles from the village, the travois suddenly stopped in the sand, and Bear Robe's younger brother cried out to Henry. Turning and galloping back, Chatillon lunged from his horse, burrowed through the crowd of Indians surrounding his wife, and leaned over her just as her last murmur quivered and died.

Later, he and Shaw returned to Bear Robe's village and sat in silence all night as a triple line of Sioux mourners circled the fire, passed the pipe, dwelt on her spirit, released neither tears nor joy.

As June passed, Chatillon grieved his loss. Parkman and Shaw tried to chart the movements of the Sioux around the fort, hoping they could definitely pinpoint the location of at least one large village. By the first week of July Parkman was concerned that his dysentery would prevent him from searching for the Sioux and that the whole expedition would end in failure. He had traveled over two thousand miles just to throw himself on a buffalo rug and listen to his own pathetic sobs!

He could wait no longer. Feeling somewhat stronger, he urged Shaw to accompany him into the mountains to find the Sioux village. The exhausted Shaw (also laid up, with a case of poison ivy) declined. Parkman grabbed a pumpkin-headed Canadian named Raymond from the fort and told him to prepare for an arduous ride. As they departed, Parkman told Shaw that he would be back by the first of August.

And so Raymond and the still wobbly Parkman headed south to find the Sioux. They crossed rolling prairie laced by creeks feeding the Platte. Broad- and narrow-leafed cottonwoods clustered by the stream beds, and as the land rose into the Laramie Mountains, pine forests replaced the deciduous canebrakes. The sun beat down. They searched the ground for tracks, yet kept a wary eye on the uneven horizon.

Toward mid-July, close to forty miles southwest of Fort Laramie, Parkman felt human again. He could ride without swaying and eat without throwing up. On the banks of Laramie Creek Raymond found a moccasin print. A little farther on they discovered the prints of horses, men, women, and children. For two days they tracked the Indian band, frequently losing the trail as it went up through the stony soil of the mountains. Finally they gained the top of a forested ridge. Staring over the ragged treetops, they saw a lush valley below and the cloud-shrouded Medicine Bow Mountains looming over it. They pressed on and Parkman again looked at the valley floor, focusing on several moving black dots.

"Buffalo!" he shouted.

Raymond stared. "Horses, by God!"

They had found the village.

Parkman and Raymond spent nineteen hectic days in and around the Oglala Sioux camp. Who would have thought of it?

Who would have dreamed it — a Harvard LLB, accompanied by a half-witted nomad, completing his rite of passage among savages at the foot of the Medicine Bow Mountains. But this is what he wanted, what he had come over a thousand miles for: a peep at Sioux life, a look at ritual and "barbarism," anything non–New England. He didn't need to be a snob here. They wouldn't let him. He could simply be white and afraid, watching and saying very little. He would tell everyone when he got home. If he got home.

Big Crow, a man of sinuous strength and enormous capacities for food and drink, was the chief of the village. Parkman and Raymond were brought to his lodge by several warriors. Reynal, a white trader from the fort, was in the village with his Indian wife and acted as interpreter. Squatting on his buffalo rugs, Big Crow greeted his visitors and reached for his pipe, filling it with a mixture of tobacco and kinnikinnick. They smoked and ate boiled buffalo meat together. Soon other warriors filed in, staring at the two strangers and acknowledging Reynal. Parkman mustered his courage and stifled any sign of fear. He was to describe the conversation that followed in *The Oregon Trail*. "I had come from a country so far distant," he told the men, according to his account, "that at any rate of travel, they could not reach it in a year.

"How! How!" the warriors chanted.

"There the Meneaska were more numerous than the blades of grass on the prairie. The squaws were far more beautiful than any they had ever seen, and all the white men were brave warriors.

"How! How! How!"

"While I was living in the Meneaska lodges, I had heard of the Oglala, how great and brave a nation they were, and how well they could hunt the buffalo and strike their enemies. I resolved to come and see if all I heard was true."

"How! How! How! How!"

And so it went, according to Parkman's reminiscence, as he poured sweetness and goodwill into the hearts of the fierce Oglalas.

Old Mene-Seela, the medicine man, rocked forward and told the group that because everyone was together it was a good time to make plans for the coming season. The lodges were old and crumbling. Buffalo-cow leather was needed to replace them. There must be plentiful buffalo herds in the mountains, Mene-Seela said:

if the Snakes attack we will be ready for war. And he pointed out the presence of the white men with rifles to help.

Soon the village packed up, taking down lodges and preparing for the migration to find the buffalo herd that old Mene-Seela had talked about. Horses, dogs, women, and men left the prairie in disordered caravans and traveled into the mountains. Parkman, Raymond, and Reynal rode with them.

Several days later they camped near a large buffalo herd and prepared for a "surround." The braves chose their best horses. The women got the camp ready for feasting. Old Mene-Seela told them that they were on the enemy's hunting grounds and that they should be proud Oglalas and strike the herd.

The warriors assembled in knots and urged their horses into the valley where the buffalo grazed. Moving swiftly, they descended the hill, moved through the spears of sagebrush, and leaped the tumbling streams. Parkman, again weakened by dysentery, joined the advancing throng, which became to him a blur of manes, tails, and painted bodies.

After the hunt, the meat was loaded up and taken back to camp. Parkman rode in, lurched toward Big Crow's lodge, threw himself on a buffalo rug, and slept. The piles of flesh and hides were carted into the village. The grass was bloody from the thick sides of buffalo that the women had dragged to the lodges. Into the night, fires blazed and the men howled, gorging themselves on boiled and roasted bison. Old Mene-Seela came into Big Crow's lodge and told Parkman that he thought beavers and white men were the wisest things on earth. Parkman sat up and ate buffalo with his guest. He was dazed, weak, and full of bad dreams, but he had never felt better.

For five days they hunted in the mountains. Women stretched the buffalo hides on the ground and scraped them industriously. Some of the women and children tossed a young boy up and down in one of the hides. Parkman ventured out with the hunting parties, returning to watch the diverse activities and to sleep.

One afternoon when he and Reynal entered Big Crow's lodge, they found the chief sitting, half-naked and resplendent, on his buffalo rugs. Parkman noticed the scars on the chief's upper torso, the result of skewering the flesh with wood splints and attaching heavy buffalo skulls. The chief was talkative today, bragging (perhaps lying, thought Parkman), about his exploits as a warrior. Big Crow remarked that he had killed fourteen men. He pointed through the lodge opening at the mountains. Two summers ago while traveling there, he said, his party had run into two Snake braves. They shot one and chased the other through the trees until they finally cornered him. While two men held the Snake warrior, Big Crow advanced and scalped him alive. They built a great fire and threw their captive into it. There were other particulars that Parkman found so savage, he confessed to his journal, that he was unable to relate them.

Would Parkman have stayed longer in the Sioux village had he not promised Shaw to be at Fort Laramie by the first of August? Perhaps. He liked the crude tempo and violent rhythm of Big Crow's camp. He enjoyed listening to Mene-Seela, even though the old medicine man confessed, Parkman wrote, that " 'it is a bad thing to tell the tales in summer. Stay with us till next winter,' " the old man had promised, "and I will tell you everything I know." And, of course, Parkman knew that the summer was advancing and that he had to recross the prairie by autumn. The first days of August seemed as good a time as any to leave. The village had abundant meat and hides for the lodges. The Snakes lurked in the mountains, but they had not threatened the Sioux.

Early on the morning of August second, Raymond shook Parkman's shoulder to wake him. They collected their gear, saddled the horses and, accompanied by a Sioux named Hail-Storm as guide, they plodded up the pass and into the wooded slopes of the Laramie Mountains. In the gray light of morning, Parkman looked back at the smoke from the village, "half unwilling to take a final leave of my savage associates," he later wrote.

The following day they reached the fort, where Parkman greeted Shaw, Chatillon, and Deslauriers.

"I have been well off here in all respects but one," laughed Shaw. "There is no good *shongsasha* [concoction of dried leaves and berries] to be had for love or money."

Whereupon Parkman produced a small leather bag that he had brought from the mountains. They lay on their buffalo rugs, read Byron and Shakespeare, smoked their *shongsasha,* and planned their journey home through Colorado and east along the Santa Fe Trail.

From the rampart at Bent's Fort Paul and I could see the prairie sloping away to the highway and the tree-lined ribbon of the Arkansas River. Beyond, far away in the haze, rose the pale blue outline of the Rockies.

"The rest is anticlimactic," I said finally. "Parkman's group traveled south along the Front Range, arrived in Pueblo, where they jettisoned Raymond for his unpredictable behavior, and headed for Bent's Fort. They got here, sunburnt and tired, toward the end of August. Kearny's army had been through not a month before, resting on the way to Santa Fe. The grass surrounding the fort had been nibbled clean by his animals, and Parkman and the others were hard pressed to find food for their own horses. Susan Magoffin had arrived and left for Santa Fe. The Bents were away, and a fellow named Holt was in charge. He invited the four to dinner, and that's why when I saw the table in the room below I started working out the seating arrangements. It must have sounded odd."

Paul stared across the prairie, his pipe cocked rakishly in his mouth. He said nothing for a moment. "There is one thing," he said presently. "Come on. Perhaps it's minor, but let's have fun with it."

We descended the steps into the quadrangle and returned to the dark room where the crystal gleamed and the flatware shone with a dull radiance. Several people circled the room, idly staring at the table, the floor, and the walls, and then passed out the door.

Paul stood over the table with his hands resting on the back of a chair. "You said Holt, being in charge, sat here at the head of the table."

"Yes."

"Hmmm. I don't think so. Let's play it back and see. It's August whatever, 1846. Holt stands at the door and welcomes the four as they file in. They all stink, of course, despite a swim in the river. Chatillon introduces himself and the others. Mr. Parkman. Mr. Shaw. Mr. Deslauriers. So on. Chatillon briefly relates what they've been up to all summer. The Rockies, the Sioux, the buffalo hunts, the great northern prairies. The whole bit. Holt suddenly realizes that he stands in the presence of the great Henry Chatillon, lord of the plains. Holt is pleased — perhaps overwhelmed — that such a famous man has arrived at his fort. They move to the table. Parkman stares at the feast on the candelit table: ambrosia! His mouth waters. Holt starts to draw back this chair at the head of the table. 'Ah,' he says, 'Mr. Chatillon, would you do us the courtesy of sitting here at the head of the table.' Henry, the noble Henry Chatillon, though slightly embarrassed, complies. Therefore, Henry sits here, Parkman to his right, Shaw there, Deslauriers there, and Mr. Holt on Henry's left. That's a bit shuffled from the way you had it."

"You amaze me," I said. "And I thought you didn't care for the details of history."

"I don't. I just know people."

Fifteen minutes later I was pulling my pack out of the Porsche and securing it on my back.

Paul stuck out his hand. "I'll wait for your call. Good luck. Are you on your way shortly?"

"Yes. There's one more room I have to see, and then I'm off to the highway."

We shook hands, and then Paul climbed behind the wheel, turned the engine over, and let it purr for a moment. Backing out, he waved, cruised forward, turned onto the pavement, and was gone. I watched the red hood disappear into the haze, and then I turned back to the fort.

3. The Invincible Summer

The fastest-selling book in Independence in the summer of '46 was Josiah Gregg's *Commerce of the Prairies*. It even sold seventy-five copies in one day in Samuel Grimes' mercantile — not bad for a five-and-dime in a podunk town at the head of the Santa Fe Trail. Every trader and traveler on the trail to New Mexico stopped in and bought a copy, so that at night in southern Kansas, while the wolves howled and the crickets chirped, he or she could lean close to the fire and learn of the terrain and culture ahead.

The Oregon Trail to the north continued to serve as an escape route for disgruntled Yankees, and the Santa Fe Trail to the south remained the route of business and commerce. In 1825, George wrote, Congress had authorized "the president of the U.S. to cause a road to be marked out from the western frontier of Missouri to the confines of New Mexico." Although Santa Fe was in Mexican territory, American companies had established and maintained a lucrative trade with the city.

In 1831, Josiah Gregg, then a frail twenty-five-year-old from Independence, had joined the raucous caravans heading to Bent's Fort and New Mexico. Only months before, suffering from a form of consumption that laid him up for weeks a time, Gregg had barely been able to walk across his bedroom. Watching the poor man sink into depression, his doctor ordered Gregg out of bed and outlined the benefits that a trip on the Santa Fe Trail in a wagon train might give him. The road was winding, hot, and muddy; Comanches preyed on the wagons; but it might be just the tonic he needed.

The doctor was right. Gregg developed a thriving business and spent the next nine years on the trail, completing several outbound and return journeys with various cargoes. He came alive on these trips, thrilled by the isolation, the buffalo, the prospect of going somewhere. Too often, however, upon returning to Independence he rolled into bed, cried, and slipped into lassitude again.

Out on the trail he kept a daily diary. In encyclopedic fashion Gregg listed the natural elements along the trail — animals, landmarks, rivers, thunderstorms, windstorms, ponds, buffalo wallows — and then added a few narrative anecdotes. He also reported on the social and cultural aspects of Santa Fe, including its history, government, religion, and arts and sciences.

Early in 1840 Gregg made his last trip on the Santa Fe Trail, retiring, he thought, to pursue other business ventures. It was the wrong move. He became edgy and irritable. Later he wrote, "Scarcely a day passes without experiencing a pang of regret that I am not now roving at large upon those western plains." His future at this point was predictable: years of traveling south and east in search of a reprise of his prairie years. He also worked on his book, the record of his journeys in the Santa Fe trade. Published in 1844, *Commerce of the Prairies* is Gregg's account of his courageous departure from his deathbed and gives the reader a glimpse of a windy, forlorn, wonderful, and — alas — vanished world.

Susan Magoffin bought a copy of Gregg's book in the summer of '46, and she was so fascinated by it that she committed whole sections to memory. The bride of Samuel Magoffin, she was pregnant with her first child and bound for Santa Fe.

In 1846 the Magoffin name was inextricably linked to the commerce of the Santa Fe Trail. For twenty years James Magoffin, and later his brother Samuel had engaged in a lucrative trade with Santa Fe and Chihuahua. When war with Mexico broke out that summer, James was summoned to Washington by President Polk. In June, before Kearny's march toward New Mexico, Polk asked Magoffin to use his influence to infiltrate Santa Fe and usurp from within the power held by Manuel Armijo, governor of New Mexico and commander of the Mexican forces at Santa Fe. James Magoffin left immediately for Independence and Santa Fe.

During the second week of June, or about the time that Francis Parkman reached Fort Laramie, Samuel and Susan Magoffin were leading a caravan out of Independence toward Council Grove and on to Colorado. Susan traveled sumptuously by Santa Fe Trail standards: she had at her disposal a small tent house, private carriage, her books, notions, a maid, and two servants. Her husband showered her with gifts and affection. She was devoted to him, and a large part of her diary deals with her thoughts about adjusting to marriage in a wild new land. Gregg's book was near at hand, for she was using it as a reference to mark points along the trail. Her greyhound, Ring, bounded along by the wagons, sniffing out the prairie's exotic smells and chasing rabbits and buffalo. She wrote in her diary frequently as she traveled to Santa Fe. In 1926 it was published under the title *Down the Santa Fe Trail and into Mexico.*

Kentucky born and raised, Susan Magoffin had neither Parkman's education nor his conceit; her diary reveals a gracious, accepting, often naive personality. Her wealthy parents had sprung from rugged pioneer stock, which accounts for the toughness and durability she displayed on the trail. Although it was probably not meant for publication, the diary is conspicuous in its correctness of spelling and grammar, as if the writer wished herself or someone else to read it aloud some day.

When they had pushed out onto the trail, when the towering elms and maples gave way to the flowing green prairies and gray-and-white thunderheads above, she was, as Bernard De Voto wrote of Parkman, "all eyes drinking in strangeness." Everything was close and vital: the prairies sweeping on forever, the punishing sun, the delicate flowers, the groans of oxen and mules as they plodded on, Ring yapping at a rattlesnake. By the middle of June, they were a hundred miles out of Independence and entering Council Grove, where in one of the parties they ran into artist John Mix Stanley, who was heading for Santa Fe. Good humored and outgoing, Stanley was to join Kearny on his march to the Pacific and become one of the earliest first-rate painters to sketch the Southwest.

Shadowing the Magoffin caravan virtually from the beginning were detachments of Kearny's Army of the West — a rather grand title considering the disjointedness of the march. Some of Kearny's dragoons left Fort Leavenworth on June sixteenth and straggled in the Magoffins' wake all the way to Bent's Fort. The army consisted of close to 1,600 men, among them well-drilled regulars, cavalry, and some bedraggled infantry. In separate caravans they left for Bent's Fort. The strenuous journey weakened Kearny, but he remained a model of discipline; meanwhile his men hunted buffalo at will and dispersed to gather bison chips for the fires. The heat soared, the wind and dust stung, and as Kearny and the Magoffins discovered, the water along the trail got fouler and scarcer. The infantry grumbled about the cavalry; the cavalry griped about their officers. But they were buoyed by one thing: they still had not seen any Comanches.

The Magoffins, having rested in Council Grove, left there on the twenty-first and began to encounter some of the first pitfalls of the journey: lost animals, stuck wheels, waterless creek beds, famished mosquitoes, collapsing wagons, and thrashing downpours. But what of it? Susan wrote in her diary, "There is such independence, so much free, uncontaminated air, which impregnates the mind, the feelings, nay every thought, with purity. I breathe free without the oppression and uneasiness felt in gossiping circles of a settled home." She said: I breathe free. She had found the West.

The Magoffins arrived at Bent's Fort on July twenty-sixth, two days before Kearny's army pulled in. For several weeks Susan had been sick. As her pregnancy had advanced, her health had declined, exacerbated by the jolting ride, the heat, and the fickleness of the weather. She had lost weight. She immediately went to her room, a dark, smelly place with crude furniture and a dirt floor.

There was a single bed with a stand and washbasin, and a narrow opening to the light outside. Susan was terribly weak and pale, but the place with its close darkness and coolness must have looked inviting in contrast to the sun and heat outside. Luscious darkness. She slept.

Samuel came in and held her hand. A doctor named Mesure gave her pain medication. She rose the next morning, still shaky, and hobbled around the fort and down to the Arkansas. Near the quadrangle she was surprised to find "a regularly established billiard room! There is no place on Earth I believe where man lives and gambling in some form or other is not carried on," she observed in her diary.

On the twenty-eighth and twenty-ninth of July, Kearny's forces straggled in. Suddenly the fort rang with the din of horses and men, wagons and howitzers, rattling sabres and blaring trumpets. On the thirtieth, bedridden and in pain, Susan could hear the clamor in the yard beyond, blacksmiths nailing shoes onto whinnying horses, children crying, men swearing, mules braying, servants bickering. It was her birthday, and she was sick!

The next day her condition worsened; she went into premature labor. Samuel and Dr. Mesure rushed into her room. Mesure soothed her with medication and waited by her bedside. On and off through the night, pain seized her thin body. Samuel took her in his arms. Near midnight she miscarried and, after weakening rapidly, dropped off into a heavy sleep.

Over the next few days she shunned self-pity, relying on her deep faith. She lay in bed and heard the musterings of soldiers outside; she thought of the futility of war and the higher purposes that people should pursue. She was amazed and delighted that an Indian woman in another part of the fort had given birth to a healthy baby and within half an hour was bathing in the river. She harbored no resentments, railed against no gods. She became happy about the future with her husband: on to Santa Fe.

Meanwhile, Stephen Kearny staggered around Bent's Fort, weakened by the arduous march from Leavenworth. He held brief meetings with his staff, conscripted more men for his army, drilled his dragoons on the surrounding prairies, and prepared his memorandum to Manuel Armijo. In his note, Kearny was gracious but firm, employing a diplomatic tone that makes murder and friendship sound like bedfellows. He wrote that he had a "strong military force" set to enter New Mexico and that the governor would be wise not to take arms against it. He also warned the people of the region to "remain tranquil." (Remain tranquil! Pardon me and my government while my army takes your country away from you.) He signed the letter on August first and dispatched Capt. Philip St. George to Santa Fe to deliver it. By the following day, when Kearny led his cavalcade onto the Santa Fe Trail, everything seemed to favor a quick surgical removal of a large chunk of territory from Mexican control.

Four days later, on August sixth, the Magoffins left Bent's Fort, bound for Raton Pass and New Mexico, hoping to travel in the relatively safe wake of Kearny's march. They crossed the Arkansas River into Mexican territory. Suddenly the fort receded into the waving heat, the river stretched ahead through its banks of cottonwoods, and beyond the prairie rose steadily to New Mexico. They were all alone again.

꩜

In the late afternoon sunshine I loaded up to follow their path. I left the quadrangle with its dwindling masses, noisy blacksmiths, and steadfast pioneer women and headed down the prairie to the river and the trail. I was still haunted by the sight of the small, dark room I had visited after Paul had left. Susan Magoffin's presence there had been almost palpable. I didn't just imagine it — I *knew* this was the room where Susan had lain. With the fort's sounds still chiming in my ears, I crossed the grass knolls, absorbed by that bold American summer of '46, lost in its people and its oxen, its pots and pans and creaking wheels.

There wasn't a cloud in the faded denim sky. The heat continued to rise off the prairie, but down by the Arkansas a vaporous coolness hung over the current. Locusts shrieked in the tall grasses. It felt awkward at first to be walking again, but after about half a mile I found my natural stride. The pack suddenly felt comfortable, my legs were strong, and the trail ahead seemed secure as it snaked along the banks of the river. I ate squirrel food from my pack.

The trail follows the Arkansas west for six miles, and then at La Junta it turns southwest to cross the rangelands leading to Raton Pass. The Arkansas is no Mississippi or Missouri, but it does have a formidable current. It was muddy and bank-full from spring runoff in the Rockies. In the shallows under the trees there were eddies where a horse or ox could wade and drink protected. Farther upriver were spots where a whole herd of antelope could cool themselves. But there were no animals to be seen that afternoon. I only heard the river, the locusts, and my own footfalls.

I camped by the river near La Junta, gathered wood, and got a little fire going. I heated water in a pan and made instant coffee. I nibbled more squirrel food. A fresh breeze rose off the river and wafted down the bank, the soothing wind that usually swirls in at twilight and cools the stones of the shore. I put my hands around my tin cup and took stock of things.

The Magoffins were ahead of me. No problem, I thought. I could make up the distance tomorrow. I didn't even know if camping here was allowed, but I felt a strange rightness about the place: the tent of cottonwoods, the hum of the river, the red ants who scurried industriously after a human body had plunked down in their sacred country, and the dirt that felt cool and supple.

I shook out my ground cover and unrolled my sleeping bag

onto it as the stars began to peep down. Some readers may think at this point that they are in the presence of a happy camper. Not true. I could have easily settled for a bed in a motel on the highway. But early on I had resolved to make this as authentic a journey as possible, and I was quite willing (well, maybe just willing) to encounter the discomforts that went along with it. I put my head down on a small lumpy pillow, listened to the river sing, planned my journey for the morrow, and slept.

La Junta straddles the highway, a core of traditional brick buildings surrounded by a host of fast food joints, convenience stores, and dirty garages. North of the highway a great network of railroad tracks zigzags in and out of a terminal. The pungent smell of cattle and hay hangs in the air. Of course, there was nothing here when Parkman and the Magoffins passed through, so most of the edifices are of the twentieth century.

I found a small café in the heart of town that had a lovable shabbiness. Locals were grouped in a corner, loitering, smoking filterless cigarettes, jawing and nodding. I sat at the counter, behind which a waitress in her fifties paced up and down, snapping gum and looking as though she had come straight from the corner beauty parlor where some innocent student had transformed her perfectly natural hair into a scarlet polyester nest. A country tune squeaked from the little speakers, and a ceiling fan circled at half speed. Over in the corner a small table fan, about six inches wide, blew the smoke around the room.

Despite the airless interior and the lacy green wallpaper, I knew I could get a good meal here. It's part of the American experience: good things come in awkward packages. Helen, as her name tag read, took my order and splashed some coffee into my cup. She peered over at my pack, which I had slung against the stool next to me.

"You look like you're out for a walk," she said.

I said yes.

"Where ya goin'?"

"Santa Fe."

I suspect she had expected me to say something like the other side of La Junta, for she blurted out, "Santa Fe! Good God! How far is that, anyway?"

"Oh, about two hundred miles."

"Two hundred miles! And you're gonna walk there? In this heat? Why don't you take the bus or somethin'? Greyhound goes down there all the time. Hold on, your eggs are ready."

About halfway through my meal she returned with the coffee pot. "More coffee?" Without waiting for me to answer, she deftly refilled my cup.

"You look like a toury," she said.

"A toury?"

"A tourist. They're always passing through here. Who wants to live in La Junta, anyway? They're headin' up to the mountains. They're headin' back to Kansas. Everybody's movin'. There are always two types of people in here: the locals who stay in one place, and people like you. I can spot 'em a mile away. And you're goin' to Santa Fe! Are you a Coloradan?"

"Yes," I said.

"Good. Let me give you a piece of advice. When you get back, stay here."

An hour or so later I had cleared the city limits and was walking down Highway 350, the asphalted, modern version of the Santa Fe Trail. It had dawned a clear day, but now, I noticed, the air held more humidity. I had about a three-foot shoulder to walk on, and to my left a grass gully sloped to the barbed-wire fence forty feet away. Campers, trucks, and cars whizzed past; an old Ford clunked by. By noon I had gotten used to the vehicles going and coming. On my right the Santa Fe Railroad tracks followed the road, a constant reminder that in high country the highway and the railroad together take the path of least resistance.

At two in the afternoon I stopped and put on my Panama Jack hat, a soft, cool buffer against the hammer of the sun. Big woolly clouds formed to the west and drifted lazily overhead. Meanwhile, the road stretched ahead, empty except for the silver mirages on the distant pavement.

In writing about Walt Whitman, D. H. Lawrence once commented that American literature is concerned with the open road. Perhaps this is true, and it is never more on target than for the literature centering on the American West. We have not had to endure the mystical ecstasies of the Middle Ages or deal with the spiritual battles of a counterreformation. We have little religious art because of this; we are a country of few saints, many pioneers.

Whitman, who was twenty-seven in 1846, would have been the perfect spokesman for this stretch of trail. But, alas, he was tied up with making money in the East and had not yet surrendered to his truant blood. It was a summer that saw the publication of *Typee,* Herman Melville's Polynesian answer to Parkman's sojourn among the Sioux. But Melville, also twenty-seven that year, could never travel this trail without turning back. Although he was a natural, curious observer, he loved the sea wind and the boards shaking under his feet. He cared little for dust and imperialism, for a country overrun with armies, tourists, and religious madmen. Whitman and Melville were truants. So were Cooper, Irving, Parkman, and Twain. So too am I. Only by the journey down the open road.

Away now, Walt Whitman! Get up from your warty, ink-stained desk and squeaky chair. Lift your china blue eyes West and come with me. Are you who you say you are? A rough, a kosmos, a water buffalo? If you are, I've a land to test your boasts, whet your heart, and answer your prayers. Leave the dust and murk of your old Brooklyn shanty and I'll show you this land of butte, hawk, wind, and star. Away now, Walt Whitman! Leave New York, as if you were a refugee fleeing Budapest or Berlin, and come with me, now, into this summer, while we are still alone in a naked, infant America. Begin your poem, begin your book, begin your life, now! You rough, you kosmos, water buffalo, you good gray poet, camerado, you!

Typical rangeland stretched away on either side of the road: rolling, brushy hills, no trees, large patches of sand. Wanting a rest, I left the road and tramped in about a quarter-mile, erecting my small one-man tent behind some ancient rancher's crumbling drift fence. I was just in time, for it started raining, very timidly at first, the drops like fine needles spearing the ground. A sudden coolness overcame the soil, cutting the heat in a matter of moments. Then there came a loud whoosh of air, and the rain started driving hard against the tent. I peered outside. The sky was as dark as pitch. Lightning flashed over the mountains and thunder rumbled so loudly that the ground shook. Suddenly little rivers of rain coursed through the dense buffalo grass. I could hear the wind rushing and howling over the sound of the rain pounding the green, spongy earth.

The storm lasted for perhaps twenty minutes. The wind was so strong at times that it slapped the side of the tent and shook it like a sail. The prairie that only a half-hour before had looked dingy and desolate now shone with a crisp new radiance as the sun peeked from behind a monstrous cloud and warmed the ground again. I opened the flap of the tent all the way. A prairie dog stuck its head out of its hole, sniffed the wind, and stared menacingly at this new neighbor. Hawks soared in the high, swirling air currents. Caterpillars and scorpions scuttled over the washed ground. Bees droned on the clover buds. I lay back, heard all the sounds of storm and renewal, and took a nap.

The Magoffins plodded on through the dog days of August, pushing southwest into a country euphemistically called the Comanche grasslands. They were twenty-four miles from Bent's Fort and were trying to average twenty miles a day. Grass and water were scarce; sagebrush prevailed amid the brutally level sand patches. The sun turned the land to a burnt, dusty green. Samuel Magoffin walked between the moving wagons, searching the horizon with rueful anticipation. Had Kearny's forces taken Santa Fe yet? Had the Mexicans raised an army and repulsed them? Had Kearny even crossed Raton Pass into New Mexico? Where were they? Was the trail safe ahead? What Samuel did know was that, after twenty years of continuous trade on the Santa Fe Trail, an era was ending. Would his Mexican friends remain in Santa Fe if the Americans marched in? Indeed, would they even talk to him again? The wagon wheels hissed in the sand; the men joked and applied the whip gently to the oxen. Samuel looked at Susan riding in the wagon and felt unwilling to heap his doubts and questions upon her.

As the sagebrush desert rolled away before her, Susan wondered if she would ever see her America again. She had gotten used to the lurching of the wagon, the hoarse cries of the men, the jostling of pans and coffee tins, the dust devils whirling into her face; these had provided her the security of a temporary home. But in her heart there was a strange, tingling buoyancy at being involved in this adventure with her husband and riding in the caravan to Santa Fe. God watched over her, held her tightly in the palm of his hand. What was there to fear?

The sun, which had hit them obliquely until they reached Bent's Fort, now swung into the southern sky and struck them full in the face. Wide-brimmed hats and sunbonnets helped cut the glare, but there was no removing the desert mirages that trembled on the sand in front of them. She consulted her copy of Gregg's book, which counseled her that the mirages were "the effect of refraction upon a gas emanating from the sub-scorched earth or vegetable matter."

The next morning she saw two mountains rising on her right — Wah-to-Yah, the Spanish Peaks — and they lifted her spirits. The drab desert had broken into rolling, stony hills with sudden rock spurs. Farther on, the hills increased in size and number and were studded with piñon and juniper. They searched for water to slake their thirst and the thirst of their animals. At Hole in the Rock, they brought the wagons together, camped, and indulged in the only water for fifteen miles.

That night the oxen broke loose, and Susan and Samuel awoke to find themselves stranded. While the men tracked down the animals, Susan rolled up the tent windows, sat back with her husband in the hot, windless shade of the wagon, and ate roast rabbit and sipped wine. They encouraged each other. Two months out of Independence and yet another delay in the caravan! Patience! they murmured.

By August thirteenth they had reached the Purgatoire River, nearly seventy-five miles from Bent's Fort. Large cottonwoods, grassy banks, and fresh water greeted them. They rested and renewed their hearts by the river — with good reason. Just beyond the cottonwoods began the winding, tortuous, fifteen-mile ascent over Raton Pass into present-day New Mexico. A soft rain fell, cooling the air and dampening the thick layer of dust on Susan's face and hands.

Meanwhile, one hundred miles to the south, beyond Samuel Magoffin's vision, Stephen Kearny's army was approaching the town of Las Vegas, New Mexico, poised to swat a little mosquito in its way.

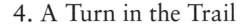

4. A Turn in the Trail

Heading southwest, I began to feel the effects of the staggering sunlight. My eyelids felt like jaws clamping shut. Frequently I had to stop to close my eyes for comfort. Even a good pair of sunglasses failed to ward off the waves of light. I kept on, stride after stride, like a madman hypnotized by the eternal horizon.

I was walking a good two feet off the pavement when from behind me I heard a huge, roaring sound of tires eating asphalt. Quickly the sound became a car screeching to a halt nearby. I turned halfway and saw a man leaning out of the car window, alternately looking at me and at his rearview mirror. He was fifty-five or so, with shorn reddish hair.

"Where ya goin'?" he said.

"The border," I said with some reluctance.

"Want a ride?"

For a moment I stood in my tracks, viewing the grim landscape and feeling the heat rising through the soles of my shoes. My legs ached and I felt gritty, sunburnt. I almost said no. Almost.

"Where are *you* going?" I asked.

"Trinidad."

Moments passed. He continued to lean out the window of his big, destroyer-class '86 LTD.

I looked down the empty road, knowing that I'd better make up my mind quickly.

"All right," I said.

I ran over to the side of the car, slid my pack off, and threw it in the back. I settled into the plush front seat. The man floored it, making the tires squeal and sending up a bright blue plume in our wake.

We said nothing for a while. The air conditioning rattled in the vents and pressed us against our seats. I gingerly rubbed my cramped legs.

"Sore, huh?" the man observed.

I noticed his hands on the wheel. Big moist hands, holding the wheel like a baby.

"So, tell me," he said presently, "what brings you out on this stretch of road? I don't see many people out here — ever."

"I'm a writer. I'm going to Santa Fe on business."

"Santa Fe, huh? You're a writer? Never met a writer before. What are you writin' about?"

"This place."

He scanned the whitish wasteland. "This place? What the hell's goin' on here?"

"This *is* the Santa Fe Trail?"

He beamed. "You're damn right it is! You know, you're one of the first persons I've met who knew that. That's right. That's good. I'm so damn proud of this place. Everybody thinks I'm crazy, but I don't care. Name's Cal. What's yours?"

I told him.

He held out a fleshy hand. "Well, it's a pleasure. Damn straight. I'm glad there are still folks around who care about the past."

We flashed by Thatcher, Colorado, which is nothing more than a single bleached shack collapsing into itself. It was at this point on the trail that Susan Magoffin first saw the Spanish Peaks.

Cal touched my elbow and grinned. "Say, I bet I know why you're walkin' to Santa Fe: to avoid all the damn traffic on the highways. Can't say that I blame you. Why, hell, last week comin' down from Denver I spent a good two hours sittin' in traffic on the interstate. Some jerk rolled his semi right on the dotted line. I mean, right on the dotted line! There I waited, drummin' my hands on the wheel. It's a good thing I had *Duel at Apache Canyon* with me. Plugged that little sucker in and listened to the last three chapters. At that rate, I could have walked to Trinidad and been there sooner. I bet that's why you're walkin'."

"That's one reason," I said diplomatically. "The other reason is that I'm following some routes of the nineteenth century and wanted to see what the countryside looked like."

"Nineteenth century, huh? You mean Kit Carson and those boys? Well, I'm proud to tell you my family's been in these parts for close to a hunderd years. Right at Trinidad, close to the Purgatoire River. 'Picketwire,' some people call it. Can't stand to hear it called 'Picketwire.' Pur gah twah. There. Never could get that French down pat, but sure is better than 'Picketwire.' Anyway, I'm real proud of this place and my folks who settled here." He patted his generous stomach. "Makes me feel warm right here."

Cal took off his sunglasses and wiped them on his sleeve. "Take my great-grandaddy. I know he had somethin' to do with Santa Fe, but I don't know exactly what. Now, there's some hell-raisin' history there for anybody interested."

"What do you mean?"

"Well, hell, I'm not sure what I mean. It's like a big family secret. Nobody really wants to talk about it. All I hear is bits and pieces. Mama knows. All I know is that grandaddy grew up at Bent's Fort, back thataway, and went to Santa Fe. Then he settled in Colorado about a hunderd years ago and began the ranch."

I said, "Your great-grandfather. Do you know what made him go to New Mexico?"

He pursed his lips. "Well, not exactly. All's I remember is mama tellin' me about Gabe Wiggins and how he drifted down to Santa Fe after the Mexicans were licked."

I didn't press the point. To our right the Spanish Peaks rose above the prairie stubble, and the level yucca beds had been replaced by looping sand hills covered with piñon and greasewood. To our left a vast grassland tract sloped to the even horizon. Ahead of us I could see the thick green rim of Raton Pass.

We lapsed into silence, and all I could hear was the dull whirr of the air conditioner and Cal's breathing.

After about five minutes, he pulled his sunglasses down to the bridge of his nose, peered at me, and said, "Say, if you're gonna do some heavy walkin' maybe you should rest a while at our place. On second thought, why don't you spend the night? Mama would like that."

"You wouldn't mind?"

"Hell, no! Look forward to it. You got any big plans?"

"Well, no."

"Good. That settles it. Tomorrow night when you're rested you can climb the pass. Cops'll get you if you don't watch it, though. Best time is between five and sundown. That's always a good time for speedin' and walkin'. Have you ever seen a cop between five and sundown? They're probably at some café, or changin' shifts, or burnin' daylight somewhere."

When we reached the Purgatoire River we were about fifteen miles northeast of Trinidad. Thin gray clouds veiled the sky and an afternoon breeze rose and drifted down the foothills onto the prairie. The desert had given way to lush, cultivated fields and to the clusters of tall cottonwoods that had sheltered the Magoffins and the Army of the West.

Turning off the highway, Cal took several dusty roads that veered away from town but always kept us under Raton's sawtooth ridge. We pushed east, briefly leaving the sites of Susan's and Kearny's private frustrations.

"Here we are," said Cal presently.

A two-hundred-yard-long dirt driveway threaded its way through a long avenue of anemic poplars, their shadows falling softly and uniformly on the path in front of us. Chickens squawked at our arrival and strutted out of the way. Crows idled in the branches of the poplars, their menacing dark hulks standing out against the gray sky.

After we pulled up to the house, silence fell like a stone. The crows circled overhead and departed. The chickens pecked at the ground by the barn fifty feet away. Through the windshield I looked at the house. Three dogs, sprawled in the warm shade of the porch, eyed me without raising their heads from the soft niche of their paws. The house was freshly painted white with green trim. An old cottonwood grew close to the side of the house, its shadow sheltering the roof and splashing onto the bare patch in front of the barn.

The house was not large, but it was redolent of history. It was a modified Victorian with a huge central gable, a long veranda, and a torn screen door. Two wicker rocking chairs stood like mute sentinels next to the door.

"I'll get your pack," said Cal. "Go ahead and go on in. We got Pepsi in the fridge. Help yourself."

I went up the stairs. Turning briefly at the top, I looked beyond Cal's car and Cal struggling with the pack to the barn and the patchwork fields stretching amber and green to the horizon.

I crossed the parlor and came into the kitchen. Opening the refrigerator, I took out two Pepsis, scanned the clutter of pans and spices surrounding me, and sat down at the Formica table. I waited, sifting through my conversation with Cal and idly focusing on some of the strange knickknacks people keep in their kitchens.

I heard voices in the other room, and then Barbara — "mama" — came into the kitchen and stood silently before me. I will never forget the impact of her presence. She was perhaps five foot six; she wore a black dress and had the carriage and stature of an aging queen. Moments passed and she did not speak, but kept regarding me with a cool stare.

I took a gulp of Pepsi and looked into her face. As she walked toward me, her crow-black dress whispered like dry feathers.

She put both hands on the back of the chair and said my name. I stood up and held out my hand, half in fear, half in friendship. She shook it limply and said, "Cal tells me you'd like to spend the night."

I sat down. "Yes, if it's not inconvenient."

"It's not inconvenient," she said, sitting down across from me. "I don't usually take in strangers. But Cal vouched for you."

I had reached into my pocket and was absentmindedly turning a coin over in my fingers — not a coin of currency but a special coin that I had once picked up as a good luck piece. She watched it flash in my hand.

"My husband used to fiddle with a coin like that," she said at length. "But he would flip it over the back of each finger. He was quite good at it."

Her fingers were stretched out on the table, and she continued to look at the coin in my hand. Rubbing the coin, I put it down a half-inch from her fingertips. Without speaking, she picked it up in her right hand and began flipping it over each knuckle, from thumb to little finger and back again. Her lips parted in a brief smile.

Cal came into the kitchen, and the three dogs waddled in behind him, quickly competing for space under the table. Cal leaned against the refrigerator, his belly hanging limply over his belt.

"Pack's up in your room," he said to me. He looked at Barbara. "Everything all set?"

"Yes," she said, putting the coin down in front of me. "Cal, why don't you take a couple of steaks out of the freezer."

An hour or so later, as I was sitting on the bed in my room upstairs, Cal rapped on the door and poked his head inside. "Come on, and I'll show you our little library."

We strode down the hallway, passing several closed doors. Turning into the room at the end, Cal flicked on the light and I looked around. Books lined shelves that rose from floor to ceiling.

He gestured proudly. "Well, this is it. Help yourself. Want anythin' from the kitchen? Beer? Pepsi?"

"No, thanks."

"O.K. I'm headin' to the hardware store. Make yourself comfortable. You might find somethin' here if you look hard enough." He paused and walked over to one of the shelves. "Where the hell's that Louis L'Amour I've been meanin' to read? Hmmm. Here it is, the rascal." Pulling the book from the stack, he thumbed through the pages and tucked it under his arm. "See you for dinner at seven." He patted my arm on the way out the door. "Have fun."

When I heard the door close I turned and began scanning the titles on the spines. There were two rows of Zane Grey, Max Brand, and Luke Short. Below that were the familiar covers of Reader's Digest Condensed Books. A couple of Faulkner's works stood sandwiched between Victoria Holt and Daphne du Maurier. On the next shelf I pulled out a plain cover at random and looked inside. A faint inscription read:

To Harvey, Christmas, 1956
I'm so Happy!
Love, Barbara

At first my search through the books felt random, but as I went further, lured by the prospect of finding out more about this house's history, I took a more serious tack and became a blood-hound sniffing out the family foxes. I rejected some of the newer titles, sensing that what I was after was probably a small note or letter tucked away in some aging volume. Guilt presently seized me. I felt that I was invading the privacy of the house, but I went on anyway.

I removed several more books, smelling their mustiness and fingering their yellowed pages. I fanned through each one looking for hidden letters and inscriptions. There were several of the latter, all innocent. I went on for ten to fifteen minutes, pulling volumes and screening the inside contents. All I found was a Mazola-stained map of Trinidad in a copy of the *World Almanac*.

I moved to the shelf nearest the window and repeated the process. I kept going down the shelf till I came to an unmarked, dark-blue, slender volume no more than half an inch thick, a little book whose cover I opened tenderly and whose words made me quiver inside. I took it down the hall to my room.

Dinner was served promptly at seven. We sat out in the back under two Ponderosa pines. A blue gingham cloth covered a chipped redwood table, and an assortment of ketchup, pickle, and mustard jars cluttered the surface. Barbara was already sitting at the table when I came out, and Cal was busy flipping steaks in a cloud of barbecue smoke only a few feet away.

"Cal, blow that smoke somewhere else!" Barbara snapped, waving her hand wildly in the air.

"Right, mama," Cal replied, and he moved the portable grill to the other side of the table.

Barbara was again dressed in black, this time in a top and slacks. In the failing sunlight, with her white hair combed straight back, her face had a teacup brittleness. She was sipping iced orange juice.

Cal growled as I sat down, "I got one here with your brand on it. You want it dead or alive?"

"Oh, shush," said Barbara, "and let's eat."

Cal brought a plate of steaks to the table, and Barbara began passing the potato and bean salads. I watched her cut her small steak into quarter-inch pieces and chew them with ceremonious precision. Cal, a perfect foil to her propriety, lined up garbanzo beans on his knife and wolfed his potato salad. Once in a while she looked over at him, frowned, raised her glass of orange juice, and pretended he was not at the table.

We talked about personal things — Barbara's family, her late husband, the ranch — and I told her about myself. In the breezeless chill of early evening, a warmth descended.

Presently she said, "Cal tells me that you've an interest in history."

"Yes," I said. "I was particularly interested in your heritage and how it developed here in the last century."

"Indeed." She arched an eyebrow and a quick light came into her eyes.

I went on, "Specifically, I was doing research on the Santa Fe Trail in the 1840s, and Cal had mentioned that your grandfather was in the area about that time. I became quite interested. He showed me the library upstairs, and after looking through several books, I found this."

I produced the thin blue volume that I had pulled from the shelves and laid it in front of her. Silently she put her hand on it, knowing immediately what it was and what was in it. She looked at Cal and then at me.

"Gabriel," she murmured.

Gabe Wiggins was the name Cal had mentioned. Because there was no name on the inside, I could only guess who had penned it. Now I knew.

"I hope you don't mind," I said. "I took the time to look through it. I could barely make out the words. Some are merely scrawls and notes. Most of the later dates are illegible. I was hoping you might be able to help me with it. Would you mind?"

There was a long pause.

Finally Barbara said, "Cal, why don't you help me clear the table. Let's move out to the front porch. We'd be more comfortable out there."

We stood up and Cal grinned. "How about a nice piece of apple pie to settle your stomach?" he asked.

I tucked Gabriel Wiggins's journal under my arm and balanced a collection of plates, ketchup bottles, and knives into the kitchen.

We talked till ten-thirty or so, mostly about Gabriel Wiggins. As I was turning to go upstairs, I said to Barbara, "Would you mind if I used part of Gabriel's story sometime?" She looked at me for a moment without speaking, and then she said impassively, "No, I wouldn't mind." That was all. She strode back to the kitchen.

The next morning after breakfast I took the dogs for a walk down the road that led between the pastures. It turned out that over the years the ranch had shrunk to a measly two hundred acres, but with its broad grazing meadows and meandering streams, it looked large to me. We reached the barbed wire border and turned back, the dogs sniffing and panting and rollicking.

After lunch I borrowed Cal's old Dodge pickup and drove into Trinidad. Built in terraces in the foothills near Raton Pass, the town had been an important junction on the Santa Fe Trail. Rustic adobes lined the roads on the outskirts of the city, and downtown a mixture of stone and brick buildings, steep streets, fountains, and tiled walkways gave it a curiously European look.

I pulled into a diagonal parking spot on the main street and went into a nearby Wal-Mart. Near the rear of the store I found a photocopy machine. I took Gabriel's journal and opened it carefully, making sure not to tear the fragile paper. There were five short pages of journal entries that dealt with the summer of 1846, and other pages I did not copy that covered some of the years after that. I put a quarter in the slot, gingerly placed the book face down on the machine, and hit the button.

When I got back to the ranch, Cal asked if he could drive me to the interstate so that I could resume walking the trail. A true friend, Cal!

I went upstairs and placed Gabriel Wiggins's journal in the bookshelf where I had found it. I collected my things, stuffed them in the pack, and straightened the room. By five in the afternoon I was saying good-bye to Barbara on the front steps.

"Call when you can," she said, and she meant it.

"I will. I'll let you know how the whole trip goes."

"That's a promise?"

"A promise." I held her hand briefly. "Vaya con dios." She smiled as if in agreement.

Cal and I got into the car and swung down the long driveway that led back to the trail through the mountains.

5. The Raton Pass

River Willow was a full-blooded Cheyenne from the rich buffalo country of central Colorado. She never knew her mother and father. She grew up to be a large woman with coarse features, dark straight hair, black pearl eyes, and a plump body. Her childhood had been full of warfare, brutality, and flight. When a party of trappers brought her to Bent's Fort in the early 1830s she thought that she had finally found a home. There were many Cheyenne, Kiowa, and Ute tepees surrounding the fort, so she felt part of her own nation while living in the shadow of another.

This was during the years when Bent's Fort mushroomed from a tiny trading post on the Santa Fe Trail into one of the great commercial enterprises in the Southwest. Three St. Louisans, Charles and William Bent and Ceran St. Vrain, had formed a partnership and erected the adobe fort to serve the fur industry in the Rockies and the burgeoning markets in Santa Fe and Chihuahua. Charles, William, and Ceran ruled the Arkansas River valley like feudal lords, employing their own particular talents to fit the needs of the frontier. Charles controlled operations from St. Louis to Santa Fe; William, the junior member, ran the fort and dealt with the Cheyennes and mountain men; Ceran, ambitious and swaggering, pioneered the lucrative outlet in Taos. Together they formed a mighty triumvirate, their empire stretching from the Mississippi to the Rio Grande.

Sometime in the late 1830s, Charles Bent, recently married to the ravishing, dark-haired Ignacia, brought River Willow an orphan to raise. His name was Gabriel Wiggins. He was only fourteen, and his parents had been killed in a wagon accident on the Arkansas. River Willow raised her white child like a son, and later he served as an apprentice in the fort's carpentry shop.

For six years or so Gabriel learned his trade, toiling in the busy shop under the billiard room. He fixed broken Conestoga wheels and mended fractured wagon frames. Traders heading to Santa Fe,

Taos, and the Sangre de Cristos filtered through, bartered their goods, and moved on. Gabriel became used to the regular visits of buckskin-clad trappers leading horses laden with beaver pelts, and of Kiowas or Pawnees in their bison skins stopping on their way east. The courtyard in front of him always brimmed with excitement, color, and voices.

One day in the summer of 1846, however, twenty-year-old Gabriel Wiggins watched in astonishment as Stephen Kearny's army swarmed in from the east and spilled onto the banks of the river. A young, pregnant American woman even showed up with them! Army tents soon sprouted along the shoreline from east to west, cramping the space used for Cheyenne tepees. The small courtyard teamed with blue-clad dragoons and officers, like huge Colonel Doniphan of the Missouri Volunteers. Doniphan was a charming, jovial man who, like Shakespeare's Falstaff, could not pass up a good fight or a merry time. Where were they going? What was all this fuss about? Someone said they were going to Santa Fe to kill Mexicans, and that the United States was at war.

Gabe watched, too, as the sick were brought in on stretchers to the available rooms, their sunburnt faces turned sideways, their parched tongues hanging out. Some limped, so weakened by dysentery and the glare of the sun that they stumbled and fell in the quad and lay there until other soldiers picked them up. Some of them never made it to the beds. Two drunken soldiers brawled in the midday sun. Later that day one of them lurched down to the Arkansas, swam, lay naked under a cottonwood, and died of a stroke. Gabriel's small courtyard was quickly filled with officers talking of war, sergeants barking orders, and uninvited young recruits filing through the gates hoping to cajole the quartermaster into giving them more supplies.

For Gabriel it was a dream come true. Never had he seen so many people crammed into one place or heard so many strange voices! And so, four days later, when a young lieutenant requested that Gabriel join Kearny's army to take Santa Fe, Gabriel leaped at the chance. He went to River Willow and explained that Kearny, his forces crippled by injury and disease, needed men badly. Gabe would drive a supply wagon to Santa Fe, and once the Americans had conquered the city, he would return a proud soldier. River Willow stared at him and saw the excitement dancing in his eyes.

Silently, she watched him walk away, accompanied by the young lieutenant.

On August second, when the Army of the West moved once again onto the Santa Fe Trail, Gabe Wiggins was driving his team close to the rear. If the sun had been hot at Bent's Fort, it was searing out on the vast, naked, stony desert floor. And the dust! The infantry, horses, mules, and wagons sent a perpetual cloud of it swirling around him and into his eyes and face. He pulled up his neckerchief. Ahead of him and beside him, he could see through the dust the cavalry, artillery, and infantry moving in a ragged phalanx toward the hills. Guidons fluttered here and there, and scabbards rattled on legs and saddles. It was wonderful to be part of such an enterprise, and he stifled any fear he might have had.

His youthful ardor, however, quickly evaporated, turned as dry as the alkali beds they encountered on their way. The temperature soared to 120 degrees. Water and food rations were cut to nothing. By the time they got to the waterholes, the horses and mules of the preceding detachments had churned the water to the color of weak coffee. Moreover, the animals had urinated in it, making it impossible to drink. Often wolves slunk close to the wagons, waiting for a mule to drop.

Farther up the ragtag column, Stephen Kearny jogged along amid a cadre of fellow officers. The man who had once joked with Francis Parkman at Fort Leavenworth now stared grimly ahead, waiting for more of his scouts to ride back with fresh information. He was fifty-two years old, and wrinkles had begun to crease his Colorado sunburn. His tight blue tunic was saturated with sweat and speckled with dust. Teased forward, his hair fell in foppish curls on his temples. Behind him the Army of the West thundered along, huge gaps beginning to open up between the cavalry and infantry.

Was it going to be as easy to take Santa Fe as some officers casually joked about? It would be quick and simple, they comforted themselves. Hmmm. Kearny worried now, even while the sun shone and the wind blew at their backs.

First things first. Ahead, clouds scudded over 7,800-foot Raton Pass, terrain as tough as any Mexican force and the initial obstacle to be dealt with.

The rutted trails, loose soil, and treacherous turns of the pass slowed Maj. Meriwether Lewis Clark's artillery to a crawl. Colonel Doniphan's Missourians were fed up with the whole mess. With his men on half rations, Kearny managed to soothe tempers and restore order up and over the pass into New Mexico. For the Magoffins, Raton Pass was a mixed blessing. On the one hand, its steep pine-and-juniper-covered slopes brought welcome relief from the doldrums of prairie travel; on the other, its sharp grades caused migraines for the men of the caravan. Their wagons started ascending on August fourteenth and soon encountered the wretched road left by Kearny's army.

As for me, I found that Cal was right about the absence of police around six o'clock. I strolled up the asphalt shoulder of the interstate to the right of a cavalcade of cars passing by. The variety of their license plates was a testament to the popularity of this rock defile.

I got a good pace going and I didn't look back. The sun was behind the mountains and the air was beginning to cool. Several motels appeared on my right, tempting me with their garish signs. I went on. The road got steeper and I increased my pace, hoping to cover as much ground as possible in the early evening.

Finally at ten o'clock, having traveled a good distance, I took my flashlight from my pack and quit the highway. Crossing an embankment, I scurried through the brush, followed a dirt road over the railroad tracks, and climbed a nearby hill. This, the map told me, was the original track of the Santa Fe Trail before there were cars and pavement and road maps. It was pitch dark and I was very tired. A coyote howled a short distance away, his cry piercing the silence of the piñon-covered slope. I shuddered, partly in admiration for this lone animal and partly in fear of his startling yowl.

I threw out my ground cover and sleeping bag, yawned, and presently collapsed into the crinkly, sweet softness of nylon and cotton. Falling asleep, I felt the coyote's howl shuddering through me.

I awoke about an hour later. Propped on one elbow, I lay in

my sleeping bag and gazed at the dark mountain edges sweeping away into Colorado. The lights of Trinidad glimmered beyond them. The moon had risen; it was almost full. To my right, in a curve of the canyon perhaps a mile away, a Howard Johnson sign flashed in the still air. To my left, a dancing serpentine of car headlights climbed the hillside and swung out of sight behind the trees. The white moonshine gilded the curves of the Santa Fe Railroad tracks as they rose and veered through the canyon next to me.

Stars popped out one by one, trembling, dazed, newborn. The air was still heavy with the warmth of the day and with the scent of pine and juniper. Down the middle of the sky the Milky Way ran like a bold, erratic brush stroke. Heaven. Stars. Eternity. It was one of those nights when reality fades and dreams creep through the darkness. Time becomes distorted, edges soften, imagination drifts. And as I felt the closeness of the night, several uninvited guests rose in my memory: Parkman and Shaw riding white buffaloes and smoking *shongsasha* in long Sioux pipes; Paul racing his Porsche with both feet on the dash; Kearny plodding along, pencil-stiff, toward his destiny.

And the Magoffins. It is the middle of August, and struggling up Raton Pass this day they have come a grand total of five hundred yards. Yes, yards! The men have been busy guiding the oxen up and down the rocky stretches. Precipices drop away on either side. Behind them, a wagon's wheels lock and it skids backward down the stones. Bears lurk in the trees, Samuel warns, inspiring fear in Susan.

When dusk comes, they camp. In the morning Susan and Ring climb the rocky slopes, and she stares at the winding canyons from where they have come. She hugs herself and dreams of Samuel. He loves me. He loves me not. He loves me. He loves me not. . . . In the midst of the wildness a sudden euphoria overcomes her. "Would I exchange this home for any I ever saw?" she would later write in her diary. "There are dear friends behind me . . . but there are ties here as strong, a link that binds me to this spot [and] till it is removed may I never leave it."

A Santa Fe freight rumbled by at two in the morning. I dozed until five, then got up, ate, washed, and returned to the highway. While I plodded on with the determination of a desert camel, the Magoffins were always ahead of me. Samuel had left the caravan to hunt game in the surrounding passes, returning with turkey and rabbit. While there was a delay on the impassable trail, Susan had rambled over the stony ridges and viewed the magnificent vistas. Briefly she had been a child again, happy, impulsive, free.

We were now at 7,700 feet, about a hundred feet below the summit. My lungs were demanding more air, and my heels were thudding on the ground. I glanced up to see several vehicles pulling into the weigh station at the top. The Colorado flag fluttered above the lines of trucks and rental vans; just beyond, the New Mexican flag rustled in a downward breeze.

As I descended into Raton, New Mexico, I began pondering one of the sober realities of my trek: the seventy-five-mile stretch of road between Las Vegas, New Mexico, and Santa Fe was prohibited for pedestrians. And since I wanted to stay on the Santa Fe Trail, this raised a provocative problem.

It perplexed me for a full hour as I paced along in the windy sunshine. Surely there was a solution to this dilemma. Ahead of me the soft green folds of the mountains dwindled into the rolling umber prairies of New Mexico. Beyond, several buttes rose in perfect symmetry through a mist more imaginary than real. . . . I returned to the problem at hand. Hitchhiking was out because I wanted a firm plan in mind before I left Raton.

When I reached the touristy outskirts of Raton, things began clicking. I thought of taking a bus, and more extravagantly, of hiring a taxi. I dismissed both these possibilities quickly. However, I had heard of car rental places that often contracted with people to deliver cars to specific points. This seemed the most logical and feasible idea, since I could travel the route and stop where and when I wanted. I carried this notion into a gas station just north of town and found one of those enclosed telephone booths that people used to set world records by piling into.

Often I have tramped several miles hankering for a good

telephone book, only to find an empty cardboard cover with somebody's gum on it or phone numbers scrawled in nail polish. This time, however, I was in luck: it was a spanking new edition. I thumbed through it, found the number for Las Vegas information, and put a quarter in the phone. A squeaky voice rose from the other end. "What city, please?"

"Las Vegas. I'd like the listings for any car rentals in the area."

Pause.

The voice returned: "I don't have any listings for car rentals in the city."

"O.K.," I said dejectedly, and hung up.

I opened the door and went outside, staring stupidly at my pack as if a kind of childish whim had been squelched by fate.

I started walking south, paralleling the highway, my head a jumble of ideas and intuitions. I once read that the definition of insanity was doing the same thing repeatedly and expecting a different result. To avoid facing this issue, I silently reminded myself that if the Magoffins, Gabe Wiggins, and Stephen Kearny could make it to Santa Fe, so could I.

A half-hour later, another light bulb flashed in my brain and I found another phone.

"What city, please?" asked a male voice.

I told him. "I'd like the numbers for all service stations and garages."

I copied several numbers, and when he reached the end of the list he paused.

"There is another listing," he said, "one for antique car restoration. Would you like that one too?"

"Sure," I said, jotting down the number.

I finally had a good list and began calling the numbers. My approach was simple. I asked the manager if, by the time I arrived in Las Vegas next week, he would have any cars to drive to Santa Fe. The first ten numbers proved to be dead ends, and I ran out of coins. I went into the 7-Eleven, changed several dollars, and put another quarter in the phone.

It was hot, and the sun seemed to focus on my neck. The phone buzzed five or six times. A little bead of sweat, prompted more by nerves than exertion, formed on the bridge of my nose and began to wriggle toward the tip.

On the ninth ring a little dry voice rattled in my ear. "This is Merlin. What can I do for you?"

"Is this Merlin's Car Magic?"

"Yup. This is Merlin. What can I do fer ya?"

At first I had thought the name Merlin was simply a device to lend an air of sorcery to the car restoration process.

"Your name is Merlin?" I insisted.

"Yup. You gotta car you wanna bring in?"

"No. I'm not bringing anything in. I'm in Raton right now and I was wondering if you've a car you might want driven to Santa Fe or thereabouts." I told him my name and what my reasons were.

There was a long pause, as if his attention had been diverted by something else. "Hold on," he said. I could hear the phone drop and the tread of footsteps in the noisy background.

Two or three minutes later he came back to the phone and said, "You wanna drive a car to Santa Fe?"

"Yes."

"I may have something for you. When are you comin' in?"

"Next week, around Friday."

"Friday, huh? I don't know if I can have 'er ready by Friday. I gotta guy's little 'Vette who lives in north Santa Fe. I think he's out in L.A. or someplace and wanted one of us to drive it over to his house. If you're goin' there, I don't see any reason why you couldn't drop it off."

"I could wait a day or two for it to be ready," I said eagerly.

"O.K. Let me get a pencil and take your name. Give me your driver's license number and a credit card number."

I read the numbers and he gave me directions to his shop, which I jotted down on the photocopied edges of Gabe Wiggins's journal.

"See you next week," he said.

"I'll be there," I said, and hung up.

I had walked into the 7-Eleven with few hopes, but as I left I felt a new spring in my step. I was about one hundred miles from Bent's Fort and 150 miles from the capital of New Mexico. I veered toward the south, saw the Santa Fe Trail swing into view, and sensed that most of the cards that had appeared shuffled and confused were at last falling into place.

6. Nuevo Mexico

The Army of the West was one hundred miles south of Raton Pass, near the Mora River. Fearing the presence of Armijo's forces at every turn, Kearny had broken his army into several detachments and had ordered them to scour the terrain as they moved southward.

One of these detachments contained Gabe Wiggins. The men broke from the army's huge dust cloud in a ragged formation, teamsters, horses, mules, and mounted dragoons pressing forward into the narrow canyon where the Americans thought the enemy lay waiting.

Feeling a rock in his throat, Gabe lashed his mules into the confusion, joined by several wagons bearing cannon. He clutched the reins in one hand and gripped his trusty caplock in the other, keeping his eyes on the captain, who was midway through the advancing cavalry troop, his arm raised, barking orders. The bugler sounded "trot," and suddenly the terror of the moment seized Gabe. This was it. This was battle. The thud of hooves, the shouts of the captain, and the glint of sun on the raised sabres seemed to express the chaos and fear inside him. Too scared to do anything else, he plunged forward and joined the galloping mass of troops and wagons.

The captain urged them headlong into the canyon. The rock in Gabriel's throat fell into his belly. He was going to die. He was going to feel what a lead ball felt like. Hot and quick.

He loosened the reins as the troops and wagons rounded a corner. The wind cleared the air long enough for him to see that the forward troop was grinding to a halt, the horses gamboling in a circle of dust. The captain's arm was raised, indicating "cease fire." Gabriel reined in his mules, and the other wagons clattered to a stop in the sunshine angling through the canyon. In a moment a great hush fell.

A sergeant rode back and told Gabriel and the other drivers to close up the formation. Where was Armijo? Where were the Mexican warriors hiding in every canyon and creek bed? A half-hour later the word came down: the enemy had retreated to the pass outside Santa Fe and were fortifying it against the American advance. More frustration, thought Gabriel. But at least he was alive.

Meanwhile, Kearny gathered his forces. In an undulating blue swarm the army straddled the rolling prairies for close to three-quarters of a mile into the distance. They were on the southern flank of the Turkey Mountains, with the Sangre de Cristos in the distance. With Colonel Doniphan, Major Clark, and his other officers around him, Stephen Kearny stood on a hill, staring southward toward Las Vegas. The scouts had been coming in with such conflicting information that his brain was awash. The "small" defensive Mexican force had grown to one thousand, then five thousand, and from some reports ten thousand men. Kearny dismissed his officers to return to their companies and prepared to move his army toward Santa Fe. Inwardly, though, he fretted: the mosquito had become a very large, elusive bumblebee indeed.

Las Vegas was peaceful when they arrived. The army threaded through the lanes of the yawning village, wary of any townspeople who might arbitrarily take up arms. Gabriel guided his wagon to the southern outskirts of the town and waited there with the other teamsters. Behind them the roads lay rutted and churned to mud by the passing troops.

In the middle of town, Kearny climbed onto the roof of a crumbling adobe, and with an alcalde and a priest by his side he told the villagers that he meant them no harm and that he could protect them from the Apaches and Navahos. Impossible. But Kearny's voice rang with confidence and authority. He scrambled down and mounted his horse. So far, so good.

As the soldiers' fires blazed above Las Vegas, word passed throughout the camp that night that the path all the way would be bloodless. Some disagreed, offering gory yarns of Mexican treachery. It was the middle of August, and for some optimists in camp the path to Pecos Pueblo and Santa Fe was paved with the gold of the conquistadors.

The army returned to the trail that led to little San Miguel, where more bewildered citizens offered them chickens, eggs, and tentative goodwill. Kearny repeated his promises to the people. When the local alcalde declined to take an oath of allegiance and preferred to await the fall of Santa Fe, Kearny stood in his face and barked, "It is enough for you to know, sir, that I have captured your town!" Admonished and outnumbered, the man complied.

The Army of the West had tramped nearly nine hundred miles in two months and had met no armed resistance. Behind them were the scorched plains of southern Kansas, Bent's Fort, the Colorado kiln, Raton Pass, the many New Mexican villages, the false alarms, the whole nightmare of the campaign on the one hand, and the disarming ease of it on the other. Santa Fe was forty miles down the trail, and not a Mexican scabbard shone in the bright light between.

For Gabe Wiggins, it had been a trek filled with fear and boredom. By now he was tired of mending broken wheels and wagon frames. Enough fixin' things, he thought. Enough. Enough. Enough. When will I get a chance to fight?

Stephen Kearny, the great white hope, the redeemer of Montezuma's and Coronado's vanquished races, hoped never.

ᘓ

Crossing Raton Pass signals the beginning of a new life with fresh spaces. I'm sure a geologist could explain this in scientific terms. But simply speaking, from western Kansas and into southern Colorado you are a prisoner of sand, creek bed, rolling horizon, crusty hogback, and the hot pour of the prairie sun. Only the skies change. And without a few salient landmarks, you begin to doubt your direction and destination. Only other travelers coming up the trail, or the conversation of your spouse or partner, or even the sweating warmth of the oxen and horses afford you a semblance of communion with the rest of the world. Your adrenalin runs on the pulse of the caravan. Days flicker and go. Nights shine and pass into buttermilk-sky mornings. Lulled by the wagon ceaselessly rocking over the ruts and stones, you surrender blindly to fate, at least believing that the trail winds somewhere, that the Comanches and Apaches are peaceful that day, and that you are indeed alive.

But after you climb Raton Pass and look down on the purplish-green countryside, on the slanting bars of afternoon sunlight and sloping buttes, on the measurable distances and indolent clouds, you feel you have entered a divine kingdom. How does

Nikos Kazantzakis say it? "We have brush and colors — paint paradise and in we go."

Amid such splendor, the Magoffins, weary from their trip over the pass, were reluctant to venture any enthusiasm. They were four to five days behind Kearny. They crossed several creeks feeding the Canadian River. The temperature had dropped twenty degrees since they had left Colorado. A light rain fell as they advanced, and Susan noticed that the Sangre de Cristos, to their right, were dusted with snow. Snow in August! Only in the Rockies!

They traversed the Turkey Mountains, undulating hills studded with juniper and piñon and carved by arroyos. Camping near Ocate Creek, they learned of bears that lumbered down from the Sangres and rummaged through campsites. With her girlish imagination racing, Susan quivered in her blankets and inched toward the fire.

By the twenty-fifth of August they had reached the Mora River and found a village. Even though these were the first towns they had seen since leaving Kansas, Susan shuddered and confided to her diary that she found them "a fit match for some of the genteel pig stys in the States." For the first time she saw the stick fences and crude adobes that were to typify the villages in the rest of her wanderings through the Southwest.

Under a wide blue sky they soon neared Las Vegas. From a hill they could see the town below set in a shallow impression in the prairie. The Sangre de Cristos formed a snowcapped backdrop in the distance.

The Susan Magoffin who arrived in Las Vegas was not the same young woman who had lain afraid and anguished at Bent's Fort only a month before. She had become confident, assured, frisky — even daring.

Donning her veil and a fancy dress she had lugged all the way from Independence, she went with Samuel into the village and attended a dinner given in their honor in one of the large adobes that stood aloof from the twisted, mean roads of the town square. Naked children and dogs cavorted around their carriage as they drove up. Inside, Mexican women dressed in chemises and rebozos scurried about the house, breast-feeding their babies in the kitchen, babbling to Susan in rat-a-tat Spanish, and smoking *cigarritos* (little cigars) over the smoking ovens and boiling kettles. Susan did her best to swallow her Kentucky propriety, and she spoke to them in broken Spanish. At last dinner was served: meat, chile verde, and onions, scooped up and eaten with blue corn tortillas. Recoiling from the pungency of the meat sauce, she plodded through the meal, smiled, and let the clock tick away. After dinner, with merriment abounding in the hacienda, she and Samuel went to their carriage accompanied by a host of people and dogs. Although she was appreciative of their efforts, she chafed on the carriage ride back to camp to be out on the soundless prairie once again.

Her heart was alive out there, nourished by the straightforwardness and lack of pretension. Every mile of their journey bore out this simple truth. Not only had she become used to the pitch and roll of the wagon and the sun searing the vacant grasslands, but also she had fallen in love with this wild life. The land east of the Mississippi was just a memory — at times, even a blur. Ahead, beyond the snaking turns of the cobalt-blue Sangre de Cristos, lay more promises of the love, adventure, danger, romance, wonder, and vastness that had already started to settle into her bones. She clutched her copy of Gregg close to her. As the land rolled away, she was at peace.

They creaked into San Miguel, which was just outside the pass into Santa Fe. More running dogs and naked children swirled by their wheels. It was the twenty-seventh of August. They received word that Kearny was safely inside Santa Fe and that the American flag was flying over the city. All was safe. While local carpenters mended one of their wagon tongues, Susan slipped away from the caravan and talked with some villagers, gracefully sharing their supper of goat's milk and stewed meat. She decided that these people and this food were not so bad after all. As she strolled through San Miguel's sun-flecked public square and gazed dreamily at the little church that bordered one side of it, she thought ahead to Pecos Pueblo and Santa Fe, sensing she was just beginning to fulfill all her dreams.

While Susan Magoffin strolled through the square in San Miguel, two hundred miles to the north at Bent's Fort Francis

Parkman was preparing to go home. He had been at the fort for about a week, and his idleness was gnawing at him.

Looking like rabble on horseback, their eyes reddened by the glare of the sun, Parkman and company plodded eastward through the prairie heat. By September first they were well up the Arkansas River. Ahead lay Council Grove, Independence, St. Louis, Boston, and a career that would make Parkman one of America's foremost historians.

As they neared the end of the trail, Parkman continued to maintain under his layers of grime the flaming snobbery that had characterized his outward-bound journey. He even recorded evidence of it in his journal. Just outside of Council Grove, close to Westport, Parkman noted, the band encountered an oncoming wagon train. The driver, keeping his team moving as Parkman approached, appeared friendly. He leaned toward them and asked, "Whar ye from? Californy?"

Parkman snapped, "No!"

"Santy Fee?"

"No, the mountains."

"What yer been doin' thar? Tradin'?"

"No."

"Trappin'?" yelled the driver, now twenty or so yards past Parkman.

"No," said Parkman, not turning.

"Huntin'?"

"No."

"Emigratin'?"

"No."

The driver finally cupped his hands over his mouth and screamed back at the uncivil bunch, "What *have* ye been doin' there, God damn ye?"

Too bad the driver wasn't a Comanche after his scalp: Parkman might have answered him.

Rain. Skies dripping since dawn, the sun a lemon wafer behind a veil of dark, sinister clouds. Tramp, tramp, tramp through the slush of the road's shoulder. Cars whistling past at irregular intervals. Horses and cows swishing tails in the lush rabbity fields at the feet of pale buttes. On my right the Sangre de Cristos protruding from the mist.

Of all the mountain ranges in North America, I think that the Sangres are among the most significant. The Tetons are more majestic, the San Juans are wilder, the Wasatch are higher, but the Sangres have a solid, spiritual presence, radiant with light, that has beckoned me since I first laid eyes on them. They begin in Colorado and sweep southeast into New Mexico, forming a picturesque edge to the Santa Fe Trail. Particularly here, in New Mexico, they cease being symbols of quest and become amiable traveling companions. Clouds descend and touch their aspen-and-pine-covered slopes. To the traveler on the trail, the nearness of their valleys signals that Santa Fe is just around the bend.

I was walking over a stretch of road that the Magoffins must have found welcome after the grueling grade of Raton Pass. The sand was coarse and pebbly, perfect for wagon wheels to glide through and make good time. The trail ran staight ahead with few impediments. Antelope were abundant. I was hiking just west of the real trail, but I could keep my eye on its course as it rambled through the wet pastureland. After leaving Raton, the wagons used to move four abreast, bearing their traditional St. Louis cargoes of furniture and dry goods. At night, the wagons were gathered into their familiar circles, the front wheel of one locked to the rear wheel of the next. The wheels were chained together to prevent a stampede of the animals during a storm or Indian attack. The teamsters would be whistling by the time they hit this region. The Colorado desert and Raton Pass were behind them, and the only things left to contend with were violent downpours, and the Apaches and Comanches.

It stopped raining around noon. Down the road a short distance lay Cimarron and the Cimarron River crossing, one of the first major fordings on the southern side of Raton Pass. I plodded through the slushy grass next to the road, then stopped to lean against a rotting post. I took off my feather-light poncho and changed my socks and shoes. By the time I regained the road, the sun had muscled its way through the clouds and poured full strength on the countryside. I soon reached a small gas station at the very edge of town.

As I approached the pumps, a tall, wiry man lumbered from the office, sidestepped some puddles, and greeted me with a grin. He wore a straw cowboy hat with a three-finger sweat mark up the crown. A sunburn crept across his cheekbones, and deep crevices ran from the edge of his nose to his chin. A cigarette dangled from the pocket of his lip, and though it wobbled and darted, it never left its niche.

"Mornin'," he said. "Or is it afternoon? Need gas, directions?" He cranked the pump back to all zeros, sized me up, and looked at my pack. "Looks like you're walkin', eh? Headin' for Taos, I s'pose?"

"No, Rayado," I replied.

He stroked his chin. "Rayado, eh? I bet you could use some grub." He motioned to the café behind him. "They're fixin' dinner in there for a bunch, but I bet if you hurry you could git your order in."

A hot lunch sounded grand. As it turned out, the café was run by the man's wife, and on this particular afternoon it was crowded with Boy Scouts and their families. The Philmont Scout Ranch was just down the road, and periodically Scouts from across the country descended on Cimarron. Every table, every nook and cranny was filled with khaki-dressed kids and their doting mothers and fathers. Coming from the silence of the prairie, I thought I had been thrust into a turkey farm.

I ordered two hamburgers and stood by the cash register. In the booth closest to me I could hear a rambunctious mother coaching her reluctant son.

She sipped a tall Coke and said, "Have you been to the forest yet?"

"We're going tomorrow."

"Tomorrow. I hope so. How long have you been here now?"

"A week."

"A week without going up to the mountains?"

"We've been practicing. I want to go home."

"Well, Harold, you can't go home right now. Be patient. Soon you'll be going up to the mountains and you won't even think of home. Maybe you could even earn a merit badge in, er — ."

"Forestry?"

"Yes, forestry! I think a forestry merit badge would look great on you, Harold."

"How's my stereo?"

"It's great, Harold. Just great. It hasn't moved since you left. It's still there: nice and safe. Waiting for you to get back. Why, you'll be back home before you know it. Now. What are you going to work on this afternoon?"

"Knots, I think."

"Knots! There you go! I can't tell you how many times I've needed to tie a knot and didn't know how. And you're going to learn this afternoon. This could be a wonderful experience, Harold! You should take advantage of it!"

Harold slouched back on the leatherette bench and stared glumly.

I took my two wrapped hamburgers outside and sat in the shade of the café. Over at the gas station, a man spread out a map on his hood and studied it. The rest of Cimarron, a ramshackle bend in the road, idly endured the blunt midafternoon sun.

I think there are as many towns named Cimarron in the West as there are named Springfield in the East. As a main village on the mountain road to Taos, this Cimarron served to collect its fair share of travelers and desperadoes. Nearby was Swink's Saloon — well, what was left of it. In its day, after the Santa Fe trade had waned, it was the center of a town eleven of whose citizens were murdered in one month. (And they wonder why small-town America is dwindling!)

At the southern end of Cimarron I found the St. James Hotel standing on the road to Rayado. All historic Western hotels ought to look like the St. James. It has a European, weathered look that seems to admit to tourists, "I will be here, God willing, despite murders and mayhem, for another hundred years." The St. James Hotel was established in 1880 and still has reminders of its nineteenth-century greatness: corniced windows, Victorian four-poster beds, chandeliers, and heavy ceiling moldings. Moose, elk, and deer heads stare down into the parlor, and over in the corner a wise-cracking South American macaw named Rainbow will take your finger off if you innocently stick it into his cage.

Down the hallway some of the notorious guests of the 1880s and 1890s have their photos hung. Clay Allison, Bat Masterson, et al. scowl at the viewer. Near them are other pictures of young men who gather at the St. James's bar, circa 1895, their Prussian mustaches dangling to their chins, their beer mugs raised triumphantly. But if you look closer, you will find these are not men. They are mere boys on holiday, with mother love and desperation burning in their eyes. Six-guns and bandoliers dangle from their rakish bodies, but their faces remain elfish, tragic, and lonely.

Other more respectable guests sojourned here, the owner was quick to tell me: Buffalo Bill, Annie Oakley, Gov. Lew Wallace (author of *Ben-Hur*), artist Frederic Remington, and author Zane Grey. But whether I looked for the good or bad, the old or new, the St. James had them in quantities. I spent the better part of an hour just poring over the registration book from the opening month in 1880 and realizing that this wayfarer's inn on the Santa Fe Trail would bring me back for another look.

Later that day I took the road to Rayado, winding through hill, brushland, and mesa country and passing near the serrated peak known as the Tooth of Time. Late in the afternoon I came upon Kit Carson's whitewashed adobe, identified with a marker, sitting in an overgrown field of grass and brown-eyed susans. The house was hand-smoothed, crude, livable. It bulged and sagged in places. The yard needed mowing.

As for Kit Carson, he was in and out of Rayado. Although he was short, he was tough, wiry, steely-eyed, and his reputation made him seven feet tall. He was a human dynamo who at any given time seemed to be living everywhere, doing everything, blazing some new track and handling some fearsome encounter — all apparently with remarkable ease. He was the mountain man's mountain man, with a dash of Christopher Columbus and Beowulf thrown in.

In 1841, aged thirty-two, he was hired by the Bents to hunt buffalo for the Santa Fe Trail trade. The next year he was with John Charles Frémont's trek to the northern Rockies. In 1845 he was in Rayado with his friend Dick Owens, erecting a house, barn, and corral with a view to retiring. He was lured away again to join Frémont's expedition to the coast, and while Susan Magoffin and Gabe Wiggins were traveling wide-eyed on the Santa Fe Trail, Carson was in California fighting, scouting, and mapping. After the Mexican War he came back to Rayado, and in 1849 he built the house that stands today. It is difficult to imagine Carson at forty settling into the life of a territorial squire amid his chickens, pigs, and sheep. But he did, temporarily. And then some other skirmish called him to Bent's Fort or Taos, and he went — nomad forever.

I had originally planned to follow the Magoffins and the Army of the West on the trail through the Turkey Mountains. Modern barbed wire and longhorn cattle, however, prevented this route, and so I detoured southeast somewhat and took a small road heading out of Ocate.

The road skirted the mountains, and periodically I had fine views of the eastern buttes. Traffic was light. The temperature hovered in the mid-eighties, and the usual platoons of afternoon clouds gathered over the Sangres. Early one day I walked through Ojo Feliz, where dogs snoozed about a foot from the pavement. Not a soul poked his head through his front door; only a far-off rooster greeted the morning. I sauntered through the southern edge of the village, pausing near the little *camposanto* to view the garlanded crosses. On one cross an envelope-sized cardboard sign read, "Pray for the soul of Marguerite, age 8."

Just outside of town I passed a rough adobe with a detached garage. As I went by, I heard what sounded like hammering, scraping, and sawing in the garage. Tempted to go on, I nevertheless stopped by the side of the road and eavesdropped for a moment. Two men were talking in Spanish, and I noticed the wooden door was slightly ajar. I translated some Spanish phrases in my mind. I paused, intrigued, trying to figure out what type of work they were engaged in. Then it hit me.

I walked up to the garage door, knocked on it, and stuck my head inside. A boy of about fourteen and a man in his sixties turned toward me. Sunlight poked through a dirty window behind them. A Chevy pickup stood to their right, surrounded by wooden chests, chairs, and desks in various stages of completion. Wood shavings littered the floor, mingling with the dust and straw.

I went through the door and moved toward them, explaining in English where I had come from and where I was going. Impassive, the man scrutinized my pack, looked at his son, turned the wooden mallet and chisel in his hand, then grinned. There's something about a pack, like a pair of leashed cocker spaniels, that instills trust. The man said, "Sit and join us."

They were both leaning over a *trastero* (dish cupboard), and the man resumed applying the decoration to it while he gave directions in Spanish to the boy. I slung my pack down, sat on a rickety stool, and watched. They went on working as though I weren't there, and I followed their movements with the fascination of someone watching the Brooklyn Bridge go up.

The bottom half of the trastero is unadorned, but the top part receives generous ornamentation. The traditional Moorish patterns — Maltese crosses and Moorish arches — have given way to more spontaneous southwestern designs such as rosettes, vines, stars, desert flora, and "bullets." I watched the man chisel out several rosettes along the cornice. He worked deftly and quickly; the surgical skill of his hands surprised me. In the end, each design had a singular character. Alas, I had to miss the final step, the painting.

The sun had sunk considerably when I left the garage. Hoisting my pack, I said a brief good-bye and returned to the road. Long cottonwood and aspen shadows fell over the track in front of me, and below, to my left, lay the valleys threading the Turkey Mountains. I cut through a tract of land and picked up the lane that follows the Mora River back to the Santa Fe Trail. Horses grazed in the deep green pastures and larks warbled over the clover buds. Ahead of me the road descended to Watrous and Las Vegas.

All in all, it had been a good week.

7. Alas, Santa Fe!

At Watrous (formerly La Junta, "the junction") two trails — one from Bent's Fort, the other from northeastern New Mexico — converge just south of Fort Union. Here some ruts are still visible that were made in the 1850s by the three-hundred-pound rear wagon wheels. By then the Santa Fe trade was truly a commercial venture, and big companies were replacing the low-budget enterprises of Josiah Gregg's day.

The July weather had settled into a familiar pattern of bright dawns, cloudy noons, dripping afternoons, and radiant sunsets. I got a ride from Watrous to Las Vegas by hanging around a truck stop and cajoling one of the drivers into taking me the short distance on the interstate. It turned out he was piloting a rickety truck laden with old tires.

On the road I asked him the question that had been burning in the back of my mind since I could remember: "Is there any money recycling old tires?"

"If there was," he said with a deadpan sincerity, "I'd stay in one place instead of driving this heap all over. The only money is in haulin' 'em."

As I thought. Another load of useless products destined for the garbage pits of America, soon to rise as a rubber mountain and join those other indispensable

roadside goodies: advertising signs, junk car lots, abandoned shacks, and shanty cafés.

I got to Las Vegas about eleven in the morning and immediately started following the route to Merlin's garage, which was somewhere above the town. Climbing a gentle slope, I arrived at a crouched, rambling cottage with a detached three-car garage. A mesquite tree grew stiffly in a brownish lawn.

I went up the stairs and rang the bell. On the third ring a man opened the door. Wearing a faded gray T-shirt and an A's baseball cap, he was of average build, with a broad, florid face, tufts of hair shooting over his ears, and three or four whiskers poking from his chin.

"Merlin?" I asked.

"Yup."

I told him who I was.

"Hey, you're early! No problem, though. We finished 'er up yesterday. Come on out and take a look at 'er."

At the garage, Merlin flipped up the door, and I stood staring at the rear end of the car. It was a shiny black '58 convertible Corvette, all right. Two scarlet flames ran across each door panel, and the body stood about an inch off the ground. Oh, hell! I muttered to myself. I have to drive this thing on the highway! Through Santa Fe! But it was only for a couple of days max, I reminded myself.

"A real toots, ain't she?" said Merlin, beaming.

"A gem," I replied, with noticeable lack of enthusiasm.

"Want to take 'er for a spin before you go?"

"No. As long as it runs, it should be all right."

"Runs like a top. I saw to that. Say, you don't know how much you drivin' it saves me time. You'll be droppin' it off sometime today or tomorrow?"

"Yes, no later than tomorrow."

"O.K." He pressed a release form onto a clipboard and handed it to me. After I signed it, he rummaged in his pockets and added, "Here are the keys and address. The owner, his name is Mr. Pennycook, wants you to leave it in the driveway so's he can see it when he drives up. Drop the keys through the mailbox in the front door."

I put my pack in the trunk, walked around to the driver's door, watched momentarily as a sunbeam flashed in a perfect pool on the chrome, and slipped into the Naugahyde seats. Putting the key in the ignition, I quickly turned it over, and the engine growled so sweetly that I decided this hadn't been such a bad idea after all.

As I backed down the driveway, Merlin crooned, "Take care of 'er!"

I smiled and waved back. I kept the top down, tiptoed through Las Vegas, and turned onto the highway, heading southwest. The wind swirled freely around the interior. I switched on the radio, pushed the speed to around 70 and sat back. The sun danced on the hood as I hurtled through Glorieta Mesa, listening to the sultry voice of the exhaust pipes.

This sudden rush of excitement surprised me. Had I forsaken walking because of the charms of a '58 'Vette? Was I ready to chuck everything I held dear for this purring, slinky thing in flaming lingerie? The sun winked. The clouds turned their backs. Not forever, I said. For now — yes.

I pulled off the highway and followed a narrow frontage road into San Miguel. I eased the car over the Santa Fe Railroad tracks, my ear straining for the slightest sound of the bottom of the frame scraping the rails. I headed for the whitewashed chapel in the plaza where Susan Magoffin had pondered her future. When I found it, I sat in the church's scrawny shadow. Letting the engine idle, I looked up at the little cross.

Wind-raked and forlorn, the ruins of Pecos Pueblo straddle the rolling foothills of the Sangre de Cristos, their pillaged, crumbling kivas open to the sun and stars. Although it is barren now, Pecos was for six centuries one of the most prominent of Anasazi communities. Crops flourished in the wet mountain valleys; deer, elk, and turkey abounded in the nearby passes; wood for building and for fuel was plentiful. Pecos was one of the easternmost Rio Grande pueblos, and although it was geographically strategic, its position near the Santa Fe Trail and the Comanche villages also made it vulnerable to outside incursion.

The pueblo had been abandoned by its last remaining inhabitants in 1838, only six years before the Army of the West rode through. It was still an important rest stop on the route to Santa Fe, for it offered protection from the elements and the Indians. Kearny's troops poked through the ruins, kicked the stones of the fire pits, and more or less behaved as huns do in conquering armies. After months of heat, dust, and the prairie, Pecos proved to be a welcome distraction for Kearny, providing him a place to give his soldiers a brief leave without the possibility that they would embarrass themselves in some foreign village. Privates, sergeants, and captains circled the kivas and stumbled up to the ruins of the seventeenth-century Catholic church built by Spanish missionaries that stood, alone and rugged, on a grassy bluff above the village. Did Gabe Wiggins join the troops in their explorations? If he did, he wrote nothing about it.

Susan, however, was enamored of the place. Clambering up the slopes, she and Samuel strolled among the ruins, and she remembered the Pueblo legend that a white god would come from the east and throw off the yoke of Spanish oppression.

As Susan and her husband walked through the church, he remarked about the nights he had slept there on his journeys. Susan's thoughts were tinged with sadness as she reflected on the decline of the Anasazi culture. In her diary she echoed Shelley: "Round the decay of the colossal wreck, boundless and bare, the lone and level sands stretch far away. . . ." And indeed, beyond the ruins on the slopes, the meandering hills to the west faded into Glorieta Mesa, and the ones to the north melted into the mountain valleys.

I bought a ticket at the information office of Pecos National Monument and walked up a twisting pathway to the kivas at the top of the hill. Signs by the side of the path warned, "Respect the rattlesnakes' right to privacy." No problem. I kept to the worn track and headed straight for the church and the great kiva. People in the crowd milling about there were murmuring the same kinds of comments that people make in Egyptian and Peruvian temples.

Between 1915 and 1925, an archaeologist named Alfred Kidder excavated Pecos, placing the date of the village's settlement around A.D. 1000 or 1100. However, Pecos did not prove to be a rich site. Its grounds yielded an odd assortment of objects: bird and human effigies, pipes, fertility stones, rubbing stones, and lesser objects such as arrow-shaft smoothing stones and a whistle made from the ulna of an golden eagle.

Perhaps Pecos's major treasure was the huge junk pile that had accumulated on its eastern edge, facing the Santa Fe Trail. For close to nine hundred years, successive generations had added to the pile, which finally became a quarter of a mile long and twenty feet deep. Like most people before 1980, the pueblo's inhabitants had had no idea that their garbage would come under such close scrutiny. The notion that some curious student might rummage through their trash midden someday would have truly perplexed and intrigued them. They tossed everything without value to them onto the pile, hoping they and everyone else wouldn't have to see it again. But the Kidders of the world made a living sifting through such garbage, piecing together the details of daily life as it was lived so long ago and putting these discarded odds and ends, neatly tagged and numbered, in museums.

There used to be a trail that led from Pecos Pueblo over the Sangre de Cristos and into Santa Fe. The Indians probably used it when they abandoned their village here and headed for Jemez Pueblo, where they took up new lives.

In 1846, however, the major trail was the Santa Fe Trail, twisting through Glorieta Mesa and leading into Santa Fe from the south. Since Kearny knew nothing of the old trail, he relied on the one that had gotten him this far. On the morning of August eighteenth, the Army of the West inched through a reported Mexican stronghold in Apache Canyon. Nothing happened. The cannon emplaced in the cliffs remained hauntingly silent as they rode past; Kearny and Doniphan scanned the shadowed crevices for hidden marksmen. Troops, wagons, and horses filed through. Silence. Thank God, thought Kearny; now, if we can just find the right method to pacify the people of Santa Fe!

It was raining steadily when the first detachments under Lieutenant Hammond entered the heart of Santa Fe. As they passed, horses and infantry splattered mud on the umber adobe walls that crowded the narrow road. People stared at the troops from behind half-closed shutters and from the rooftops. A hushed quiet ruled the town; the only sounds were the slogging of boots in mud, the squawking of chickens, and voices softly giving orders in the rain.

By the time Kearny trotted in, the rain had stopped and the sun poured onto the plaza and the Palace of the Governors. Kearny waited on his horse, looking around, dazed by the suddenness and ease of the proceedings. He then slid from his saddle and stood upright, the picture of an officer and a gentleman. A brief ceremony ensued. The thirsty and famished soldiers straggled in, lined up around the plaza, and watched Kearny approach the adobe palace.

Major Clark's artillery rumbled through and set up position just north of the city. The acting governor, Juan Batista Vigil, joined a group of citizens who greeted Kearny, and Vigil turned over the city to the American commander. They went into the palace's cool interior, where Kearny drank El Paso wine on an empty stomach. It made him silly, but it helped wash down the grit.

For the next several days, Kearny tried to organize the occupation of Santa Fe. Hundreds of miles of territory, numerous pueblos, a thousand tiny villages, and a scared city had to be administered. He reaffirmed that Armijo had fled and that he, Kearny, was in command. One report mentioned that Armijo was in Chihuahua and that his forces had dispersed and returned to their farms and villages. Kearny went to Mass. He dined with Mexican families. He smiled at the people on his rides through the plaza. Cordially and steadfastly, he kept the soft fist of occupation from becoming a stranglehold.

As for Gabe Wiggins, he joined the artillery detachment camped above the city and returned to his carpentry duties. There were many repairs necessitated by the long march, and the soldiers brought him endless work. Many of them laughed and relaxed in the drowsy sunshine, polishing their weapons and joking about the squalor of the city. For the first time in a while, Gabriel relaxed too. There were the usual rumors that Armijo would mount a force and attack any day, but he was not prepared to believe them.

From the artillery's position near the town, he could hear the church bells clanging all day and sometimes into the night. He had never heard church bells before. He asked the soldiers what they were for. To warn people to come to church, they said mockingly. All day and all night long? They must sin a lot, Gabe thought. He imagined bell ringers, padres, and people congregating, like those he had seen at Bent's Fort. The bells beckoned him, reached out and stirred his foolish blood. A week after the beginning of the occupation, Gabe Wiggins walked into Santa Fe.

Six days afterward, on the last day of August, nearly a month out of Bent's Fort, the Magoffins' wagons squeaked up the Santa Fe Trail into the plaza. Near the church, at the western end, they found a temporary home. Home? Well, it was an attempt at it: four small rooms, a shabby roof, a dirt floor, and a daily shaft of pure Rocky Mountain sunshine streaming though a southern window. The walls were cold and the roof leaked, but Susan tingled with joy.

She swept, cleaned, ironed, and organized, and as September progressed she began to shape her adobe into a meeting place of the occupation. Officers of the Army of the West visited Samuel and stayed to flirt with Susan. They talked about their experiences on the trail, and Susan noted in her diary that the officers and men were quite fortunate to have such a pious commander. They talked about their home towns and states. Susan responded with details about Kentucky and how "great men were from there or connected with [the state] in some way."

While Samuel tended to business in Santa Fe (he was quite surprised to find many citizens still backing his enterprise), Susan sharpened her Spanish with a friend of the Magoffins, Doña Juliana, and she met Dr. Mesure, the physician who had comforted her at Bent's Fort. She looked from the window of her house and contemplated the sprawling city. To the west, beyond the roofs, pigpens, and cornfields, lay the Jemez Range. To the east the Sangre de Cristos rose dark blue against the sky, and beneath them the bumpy foothills crept down to the town's edges. No matter how warm the days were, the nights were crisp and cool, and the stars blinked in the big sky. Susan found that she could walk through the night grasses without soaking her shoes. At seven thousand feet, Santa Fe was the highest place she had ever seen people living.

As September passed, a friendship developed between Susan and Stephen Kearny. One morning Kearny came calling and found Susan preparing the night's dinner. She apologized, washed her hands, and joined Kearny in the front room. Crossing one bony leg over the other, Kearny proceeded to tell her of his recent experiences in the nearby Pueblo villages. Kearny could admit to Susan that he felt out of place among the Pueblo customs and that he was always "making a fool of himself." Susan smiled, warmed by his ungarnished candor. Kearny went on to say that he saw as imminent the departure of the Army of the West for California. When he offered her and Samuel a trip west after the war, she was flattered and demure. Later, Kearny took her to the Mexican church, where she was fascinated by the rituals so foreign to her.

Kearny's visits to the Pueblo villages, made for the purpose of monitoring the Indians' activities, unsettled his placid, disciplined spirit. The Apaches and Comanches to the east were outwardly ferocious, but the Pueblos — ah, the Pueblos! They could be so calm, going about their rituals and feasts in their villages scattered up and down the Rio Grande; so peaceful, wrapped in their striped blankets and squinting at the hills, as if a quiet god had stilled the fury inside them. Yet Kearny knew, Doniphan knew, even Charles Bent knew, that resentments toward the Americans bubbled within the innocent Pueblo hamlets and that at any time they could burst into violence. Patronize them, thought Kearny. Witness their dances, feast with them in their dwellings, learn their customs, smile at them. Show them Americans are wise and compassionate rulers. It worked — temporarily.

Three days before the army's departure for California, Stephen Kearny prepared the way for his absence. He appointed Charles Bent of Bent's Fort as territorial governor — a politically astute move, since Bent's influence and knowledge crossed borders and allegiances.

The next day Kearny and Susan rode north to Fort Marcy, newly built on a hill above the city. The fort's cannon barrels aimed at Santa Fe and the great pale blue sweep of mountains surrounding the town. Kearny was proud of his gentle but firm command; Susan was certainly impressed by it too. Moreover, she was cheerful and confident. Her twenty-three-day sojourn in Santa Fe had provided her a welcome break from the rigors of prairie life, and, ensconced in her temporary home and surrounded by a host of new friends, she had blossomed.

That night, Susan and Samuel attended a farewell ball at the festively decorated palace on the plaza. This was better than all the dances in Kentucky put together! Susan gossiped with the ladies and later commented in a diary entry on the manners of some of the departing officers: "Lieutenant Hammond . . . talked of the American women, their strict virtue, which he said could not be said of the men. . . . He talked of his 'angel baby', then flew off on to the War, and almost went off into ecstacies on the subject. . . . How he happened to be in such a fix tonight, is strange, for he is a most perfect gentleman when sober. . . ." Champagne bubbled, music swept dancers onto the crowded floor, and Mexican women strolled about in their ruffled skirts, smoking their cigarritos and sharply eyeing Susan, whose shoulders were covered by a scarlet shawl. The dance continued long into the night, as the brief candle of the Santa Fe occupation burned down to the end; but hatreds between Santa Feans and Americans still smoldered.

On the twenty-fifth of September, Stephen Kearny and the Army of the West, minus Colonel Doniphan's regiment, which remained to pacify the Navahos, headed west to the Arizona desert and the conflict with the Mexican forces in California. Was Gabe Wiggins with them? I don't know. Susan Magoffin spent the day in her adobe, sweeping, knitting, and preparing for her and Samuel's own departure for Mexico. Kearny was too busy with military details to stop and say good-bye to Susan. Samuel told her second-hand. It was too bad, in a way: Kearny would never see her again.

I drove the Corvette into Santa Fe from the south along the original Santa Fe Trail. As the adobes flashed by, I kept thinking about that September day in 1846 when the principals of this narrative started taking their separate directions: Kearny to California, the Magoffins south to Mexico, and Gabe Wiggins . . . ? I realized that I had a minor mystery on my hands. As much as I had studied Gabe's slender journal, the year 1846 ended with his arrival in Santa Fe and then picked up again twenty years later in 1866, in southern Colorado. What happened in between? Barbara had told me about the particular events that occurred in Santa Fe, but after that Gabriel Wiggins's life was for twenty years a complete blank. Perhaps there were some answers here. I certainly hoped so.

I drove past the plaza and the Palace of the Governors, where Kearny had drained his El Paso wine and Susan had wowed them with her fiery shawl. I checked the address Merlin had given me and headed to the north side of town. I soon found the house, and I followed Merlin's instructions. First, however, I gave the 'Vette a fond last look, chuckling as I remembered my initial reaction to it and then wipong a few of my fingerprints from the door handle. It was, as Merlin had said, a real toots!

Toting my pack again, I walked down the street toward the center of town. I found a store, bought a Santa Fe newspaper, and sifted through the classifieds for house rentals. One of the ads read, "Share, by the week, three-room adobe, near plaza, kitchen and all utilities."

I dialed the number and a man named Felipe answered. "Yes, it's still available," he said. He added, "I hope you don't mind Chile — he's a big Great Dane who sleeps on the bed through the daytime."

It was the beginning of a good friendship.

8. Flight

When Gabriel Wiggins went into Santa Fe, he found out how quickly Taos lightning could strike.

There were many cantinas in the sprawling mud hamlet. At first, though, he toured the churches, whose bells pealed constantly, but then he joined the throngs of soldiers who frequented the cantinas, where they argued, fought, and spilled out into the street. For sheltered, innocent Gabriel, the liquor, the crowds, and the raucous behavior were too much to handle.

During mid-September he heard talk of the California expedition. He was torn. Should he go and fight with Kearny and his comrades or return to Bent's Fort as he had promised River Willow? On one hand, adventure still lured him; on the other, he realized through an alcohol fog that it was destroying him. He drank to soothe his fear and to help delay his decision.

In Gabe's favorite cantina he often saw a woman with dark, waist-length hair and a pretty face that had a certain rustic hardness to it. Her name was Angelita, and she was perhaps five years older than he. Gabe used to watch her from across the room. As she played cards with the Mexican locals, her lusty voice rose above the din of the shabby, smoky interior. At first Gabe only glanced at her from the corner of his eye while he sipped the local brew. After a week or so, he got bolder.

Through the smoke he would stare at her for minutes on end. What a worldly creature, he thought. What a shameless, fearless laugh! He had known only demure plains women, and they had become the standard by which he judged the female sex. Angelita, brazen and unkempt, provoked in him a strange, unsettling longing.

Sometimes she would look in his direction, and a dagger would pierce his heart. She was probably only scanning the faces in the crowd, but Gabriel thought she was looking directly at him. Oh, the futile hope that she would see right into his heart! Oh, the hope that their souls would connect in this dirty, rowdy place!

His heart hurt. He knew that he, a prairie waif, could not speak to her or let her into his world of wagons and sunlight. He felt foolish for even dreaming of such a thing, but the raging current of his feelings bore him helplessly along. He even deliberately stayed away from the cantina. Alone in camp, he stared over the baked roofs of Santa Fe and thought of Angelita in other men's company. The pain and anguish! Was this love? If it was, he wanted none of it. Presently he wished for anything, *anything,* to stop the agony in his heart. He stood up. He resolved go see her. Helplessly he would sit and watch her again while torment burned his soul. What else could he do? He drank to help quell the madness.

Late one afternoon Gabriel and several soldiers headed toward the cantina. It had rained in the morning, and the cavernous holes in the road were now large puddles. They went into the cantina and lounged at a table in the corner.

His heart pounding, Gabe saw Angelita across the room sitting with three men. She was smoking, playing cards, and laughing in that sharp voice that always tore at him. She did not drink. He waited for her to look at him, but she only looked at the men and at her cards. Gabriel drank, watched her with intense glances, and talked with the soldiers.

Around seven o'clock, the cantina choked with patrons, Gabriel's glances became increasingly menacing. Every laugh, every movement, every spark in Angelita's eyes made him wince in pain. It was overwhelming, this bondage to her; it was wonderful and horrible at the same time.

He watched the men at her table, and hatred aggravated by liquor swelled inside him. They drank and played with her affections; booze trickled down their chins. They lied to her and smiled. Presently one of the men stopped smiling; anger twisted his bearded face. Angelita looked strangely at him. He cursed her loudly in Spanish and slapped her. Cards and shot glasses exploded onto the floor.

For a moment Gabriel sat in shock. Then panic seized him and he bolted upright. Grabbing a pistol from a nearby table, he staggered across the room, aimed the barrel at the bearded man's terrified eyes, wavered slightly, and fired.

Confusion broke loose. Gabe heard the shot, saw people

running here and there, became aware above all else of Angelita's painful, frightened glance at him. As their eyes met, he wanted to soothe her and to kill her at the same time.

After I got settled in at Felipe's place, I went to several libraries trying to extricate Gabriel Wiggins from the dark, muddy maze of that September night. Nothing turned up. I combed several volumes of firsthand narratives of the Santa Fe occupation. They were full of information but proved unsatisfactory in my present search. Had Gabe rejoined Kearny's army and gone to California? A possibility. Had he fled into the mountains and taken up a new life? Perhaps. Had he returned directly to Bent's Fort? Unlikely, since his journal didn't indicate a settled existence after the Santa Fe incident. Had he, in fact, committed a crime? There was no real evidence that the man he shot had died. Questions, questions, questions . . .

As it turned out, Felipe worked the night shift as a cook in a local restaurant. He was usually gone throughout the day, too, and this allowed me the complete run of the place in his absence. The house was an inconspicuous adobe near the plaza with plenty of sunshine streaming in through heavy white curtains. After I made the bed in the morning, Chile, the resident Great Dane, would troop in from the yard and plop himself on the covers. He seemed to think this was his right, viewing me first with casual disdain, then curious indifference. When I returned from my explorations in the afternoon, he would roll over on his back and request that I stroke his belly. I would comply, adding some baby talk, and would then coax him — sometimes manhandle him — from the bed and lead him outside. He would go with a silent snarl on his face, plotting his strategy for the next's day tug-of-war.

Despite the frenzied exportation of blue corn tortillas and southwestern architecture and furniture, Santa Fe remains one of the great midsized cities of North America. Many observers have tried to explain this mystique, and I'm not sure my views differ much from theirs. Santa Fe not only has a remarkable diversity that springs from its sunlight, mountains, altitude, history, art, and architecture, it also possesses a splendid decay that in other cities would be considered a hideous blight.

Perhaps the best thing for me about Santa Fe is that it is still accessible by foot. Indeed, its byways demand to be walked again and again. You can go from the hushed silences of St. Francis Cathedral to the crumbling artists' hovels on Canyon Road in a matter of minutes. You can have an average meal in a posh restaurant or a great meal in a standup bar. Santa Fe is old enough to attract curious pilgrims, but it is still immature and unpredictable enough to resist senility.

As many times as I come here, I always try to find out something different than I did on the previous trip. I had been to Bandelier National Monument, the neighboring pueblos, and the studios of a handful of artists, where I had learned for the hundredth time how powerful new artistic styles here can be, and where I had seen fresh splashes of color and visionary concepts of line and form that awakened new life in me. I also had been ripped off by so-called pottery experts, so you could say the scales were balanced.

This trip, however, feeling more down-to-earth perhaps, I resolved to unlock some of the secrets of Navaho weavings, and especially to discover how the American occupation of 1846 influenced the designs. To accomplish this, I looked up the name of a shop in Agua Fria Street, just across the Santa Fe River, and went there the third afternoon of my stay in town.

I believe it was T. S. Eliot who once observed that you can appreciate poetry without necessarily understanding it. If this is true, it is also accurate about our understanding of Navaho weavings in particular and most Native American art in general. Like most people, I responded to that art before I knew very much about it, as if it spoke the language of the unconscious.

In two or three hours I learned a good deal from the man who wandered among the many blankets festooning the interior of his shop. His pale complexion and short stature made him fade into the dazzling colors and styles. He was a Nebraskan originally, who ten years ago had locked up shop in Omaha and headed to Santa Fe to buy and sell Navaho art. There are hundreds just like him, all over.

"I don't know too much about the early American influence

on Navaho styles," he explained, "but I do know that General Kearny's officers would have put down half a year's wages for one of these blankets. And when they got in a desert downpour, they would thank their lucky stars all the way to California that they had bought one. It is durable and tough and sheds buckets of water. It is unbeatable as a defense against the elements."

Before the Americans arrived, sometime around 1800, the Navahos achieved a classical style in weaving, utilizing striped designs. They learned their skills from the Pueblos, principally from the Hopis. The Navahos used natural dyes and wool from sheep introduced by the Spaniards.

Because the Navahos came to depend heavily on their blankets for trade, the weavings became known as "chief's" blankets. This term does not refer to a specific leader per se, but the tag name stuck as a reminder of their importance. The classical phase continued to use the natural dyes of blue from indigo and yellow from rabbitbrush. The early Santa Fe businessmen prized these pure, durable expressions of the Navaho weavers.

But as the American occupation extended into the 1850s, the designs began to reflect this invasion of the Navahos' and Mexicans' cultural space. Soon natural dyes were replaced by commercial ones, and the weaving process was speeded up to meet increasing demand. Tourists traveled to Santa Fe hoping to secure a quick souvenir of the Southwest. The reliance on commercial dyes and the resultant expediency of the process created the "eyedazzler" blanket — a pattern of zigzags that, indeed, dazzles the vision.

As colors changed, the designs, too, rapidly adjusted to Yankee influences. The traditional stripes, squares, and small zigzags gave way to more radical, modern motifs: steam engines, cavalry logos, and American flags. Today this process continues. The twentieth-century Navaho artist, prompted by his sense of humor and whimsy, might incorporate an eighteen-wheeler, a football, or a television antenna into his time-honored, sacred compositions.

The Nebraskan said, "The Navaho artist is quite spontaneous, but there is one thing he treads lightly with and this is the 'yeis' weaving. 'Yeis' blankets are representations of the supernatural, and some interpretations are thought to be sacrilegious. Some artists won't even attempt these designs, saving them for the impermanent sand paintings, which can be destroyed at the end of the day. Others change the image to make it religious in appearance."

Strolling around the shop and seeing the different phases of Navaho art, I sensed the continuity, dynamic qualities, and craftsmanship that have made Navaho weavings unique, ageless works of art.

Late one afternoon, I stopped by the restaurant where Felipe worked. He was almost ready to begin his shift, and he sat in a sea of empty tables going over the specials for the day. He was in his late twenties, I guessed. He sat slouched in his chair, his long legs crossed at the ankles, munching on a bowl of jalapeño peppers.

I sat down across from him and remarked about the traffic I had encountered on the way into town.

"So much has changed in Santa Fe, just in five years," he lamented. "The old part of town is crowded with cars and tourists. Water is scarce. The Californians have moved in and rents and properties have shot up. I can barely afford my little house."

I thought of the Army of the West invading the west coast, and how today the westerners were returning the favor. We talked for several minutes, and then I asked him if he knew of any interesting sights I might take in during the last few days of my stay. He hunched his shoulders and thought, rattling off a few tourist attractions in the city and nearby. Nothing sounded stimulating enough for him to elaborate on.

He took another pepper from the bowl and added, "I think there's a mountain man rendezvous coming up, if you're interested in stuff like that."

"A what?"

"A mountain man rendezvous. You know, people dressing up in buckskins, shooting muzzle-loaders, throwing tomahawks, and pretending like it's the real thing for a few days."

I had heard about this back home, but the idea that it happened around Santa Fe suddenly provoked me. I picked up a good-sized pepper and absentmindedly sank my teeth into it. "When's the next one?"

"Should be in a few days or so," said Felipe, getting up and walking over to the pamphlet rack by the door. As he scanned the brochures, I put a quick hand to my mouth, reached for a glass of cold water, and doused my flaming tongue with it. Tears welled in my eyes. Felipe came back with a pamphlet and handed it to me. "Here it is," he said, turning to get another plate of peppers from the bar. He sat down and shredded one between his teeth. "Another pepper?" he asked with a sly grin.

"No, thanks," I said, airing my tongue and reading the brochure. "It says they're going to hold one north of Taos in the mountains in about a week and a half. There's a number here to call for information."

"Go for it," Felipe said.

I rose, went over to the phone, and dialed the number. After a five-minute conversation, I made another call, this one long distance.

The phone on the other end rang five or six times. Finally a voice snarled, "Hello."

"Paul!" I barked.

"Well, hell, you rascal! Where are you?"

"In Santa Fe!"

"Santa Fe? What are you still doin' down there? I thought you'd call me when you got to Colorado."

"I thought of something even better."

"What is it?"

"Are you free in about a week and a half for a few days?"

Pause. "Let me check my calendar here. That looks good. What you got cookin'?"

"It's sort of a surprise. Can you drive down and meet me in Taos on Saturday? I'll tell you then. Bring your hiking and mountain gear."

"What are you up to?" he drawled suspiciously.

"I can't tell you. But suffice it to say I've got something going that's about as gnarly as you."

He roared at the other end. "O.K. I'll play along with you, my man. But this better get me up in the mountains."

"Don't worry, it will. Everything all right?"

"Yeah, couldn't be better. Sarah's home. Jeff, it turned out, had poison ivy. He's fine now."

"Good. See you at La Fonda around noon Saturday."

"Right. I'll be there," said Paul.

I ate a quick meal at the restaurant (something without peppers) and walked back to Felipe's place by way of the plaza. The sun was just beginning to set and a warm twilight fell softly from the sky. The plaza was still crowded with people standing, talking, and shuffling about. I found a bench and sat down, content to stare at the croud and follow the curves of the Palace of the Governors through the trees.

For the first time, I really looked at each nuance of its facade, felt myself walking across its porch and through into the interior. As night came on, a serenity and finality settled on the scene. Here, at the end of the Santa Fe Trail, my principal characters began to take their bows: Kearny emerged from the porch's shadows and swung onto his horse; Susan and Samuel Magoffin clattered by in their wagon, bound for Chihuahua and eventually the Gulf ports; Gabe Wiggins, of course, was somewhere, God alone knew where. At the window of the palace stood the remaining actor in the drama, a lonely Charles Bent, the new governor, peering suspiciously at the dark adobes and passing townspeople.

Charles Bent was forty-seven years old and stout as a cottonwood; gray had begun to streak his hair. The former proprietor of Bent's Fort was pleased — indeed overjoyed — that Kearny had selected him for this challenge. He knew the trade and culture better than anyone else in the Southwest, and he was eager to prove himself when tensions arose.

As autumn crept down from the Sangre de Cristos, Charles Bent lounged in the palace, read his reports, and anticipated a fresh set of challenges in the new season. He was alone. Kearny and the Magoffins had left. His dear wife, Ignacia, was home in Taos. Doniphan was off quelling the Navahos.

And the Pueblos were restless.

He stared across the dirt plaza speckled with snow. The Army of the West was long gone. Would the threadbare military presence in Santa Fe be enough to resist an armed revolt? Of course. Besides, Charles knew these people. At least he *thought* he knew these people.

Looking across the plaza of Bent's Fort.

Looking eastward over the rampart. Santa Fe Trail appears in the distance, with the Arkansas River beyond (not visible).

Raising the flag over the watchtower.

The dining room at Bent's Fort. Here Francis Parkman and his companions rested and dined after a long summer in the West.

The billiard room, a spot popular with residents and travelers.

Entrance to the room where Susan Magoffin stayed at Bent's Fort.

View across the quadrangle, with the billiard room to the left. Near the foot of the stairs is the fur press.

The animal corral stood at the rear of the fort. Beyond are the cottonwoods that line the Arkansas River.

Shadows and sunlight of the inner corral.

The grainy texture of the adobe walls.

The Santa Fe Trail, now a paved highway, heading south to the Colorado border.

The Spanish Peaks near Walsenburg, Colorado.

Downtown Trinidad, Colorado.

Sunset over the New Mexico landscape.

Trail marker near Cimarron, New Mexico.

Looking eastward from the Cimarron cutoff of the Santa Fe Trail.

A New Mexico mountain village in the eastern Sangre de Cristos.

The ancient village of Golondrinas, New Mexico, on the eastern slope of the Sangre de Cristos, near Cimarron.

South of Ocate, New Mexico, near Golondrinas.

Landscape near the Mora River.

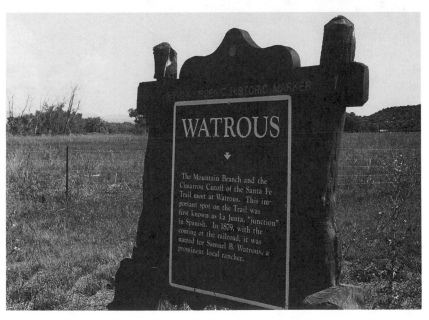

WATROUS

The Mountain Branch and the Cimarron Cutoff of the Santa Fe Trail meet at Watrous. This important spot on the Trail was first known as La Junta, "junction" in Spanish. In 1879, with the coming of the railroad, it was named for Samuel B. Watrous, a prominent local rancher.

The junction of the two trails occurred here, just south of Fort Union.

The trail disappearing into Glorieta Mesa, near Santa Fe.

The piñon-and-juniper country of Pecos Pueblo.

The Sangre de Cristos near Pecos Pueblo.

Seventeenth-century church, Pecos Pueblo.

Columns and capitals of headquarters, Pecos National Monument.

The modern trail into downtown Santa Fe.

Arts festival in the plaza, Santa Fe.

Felipe's house near the plaza.

Street musicians in downtown Santa Fe.

Facade of the Palace of the Governors.

Afternoon storm over the Sangres north of Santa Fe.

Rabbitbrush and sagebrush of the foothills of the Sangres.

Scaffolding for the "remudding" of José de Gracia Church, Las Trampas, New Mexico.

Store facade, Taos plaza.

Stairway and pots near the Taos Book Shop.

Oven and hollyhocks at one of Kit Carson's homes, Taos.

The Taos Plaza.

Kit Carson Street, Taos.

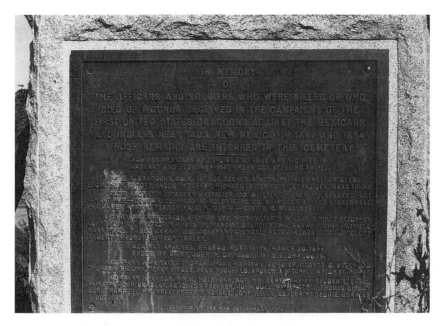

Plaque honoring those killed in and around Taos in 1847 and 1854.

Adobe adjoining the Taos cemetery. In the left foreground many of the Bent family are buried.

The Charles Bent home, Taos.

Business facade, Taos.

Looking toward Taos Pueblo with Pueblo Peak in the background.

The road north from Taos to the Colorado border.

Looking west from San Cristobal, New Mexico, just north of Taos.

Ute Peak, northern New Mexico, on the road home.

Part Two
The Taos Trail

9. God Is an Englishman

In October 1846, a solitary horseman made his way through northern Mexico along the trail to Santa Fe. On his left the Sierra Madre Mountains rose in burnished-copper and pale-blue ridges, and ahead his view of a barren, sandy wasteland trembled in the haze. His horse, Panchita, nodded along, followed by a string of pack mules.

The man was George Frederick Ruxton. He was an Englishman, and at twenty-seven years of age he might well have used the introduction "Call me Ishmael," for he had packed a good deal of adventure and travel into his young life. He had traveled in Spain, Ireland, Canada, and Africa. He was of average height, with a slight build and a handsome, almost cherubic face surrounded by a mass of curls. He hated authority and regulations. After being drummed out of the military academy of Sandhurst at fifteen he became an irreclaimable wanderer, and by the time he landed in Mexico in 1846 he preferred the most rugged of places.

Several questions are raised by this Englishman's singular journey. Why was he traveling alone through this inhospitable countryside during the war? Was he, as some observers have suggested, in Her Majesty's service, spying on U.S. operations in the region?

Ruxton may well have been a spy, but his trip was certainly not clandestine or shrouded in mystery. His superiors might have told him that since he wanted to go to the Mexican desert he might keep his eyes open and record what he saw. He might simply have been a tourist, but if so he was a very shortsighted one. Why would any tourist in his right mind travel through the Mexican desert in September and October to arrive in the Rockies during the furious storms of January and February?

A more sensible assumption is that Ruxton arrived to witness America's reaction to the Mexican War, and his role as an innocent English traveler was important but secondary. In any case, Ruxton left as his legacy a book, *Life in the Far West,* observations on the people and landscape in that volatile season of late 1846. It is a reliable, gritty chronicle, even though at times it is filtered through the sensibilities of a consummate ethnocentrist.

George Ruxton followed the trail through the rolling mesquite terrain north of Vera Cruz until he came to Chihuahua in the second week of November. He found an isolated city of ten thousand inhabitants surrounded, as he wrote in *Life in the Far West,* by a "vast territory not twenty square miles under cultivation, and at least three-fifths . . . utterly sterile and unproductive." It was a city suspicious of foreigners and braced for an American attack from the north. But using his letters of introduction, Ruxton managed to cajole the governor, Don Angel Trias, into granting him special privileges while he was in the Chihuahua environs. And so he trotted about the town, able to proceed where most members of the Mexican army couldn't go. Of the remnants of that army, freshly returned from Santa Fe, he noted disparagingly, "Their dress was original and uniform — in rags." It was this group of battered volunteers who were set to defend Chihuahua from the American invasion.

If we take Ruxton at his word (and there is no reason not to), he arrived in Mexico with superlative credentials and persuasive letters of introduction, which he produced at just the right times for the proper officials. Indeed, Ruxton bore such diplomatic immunity while traveling through hostile Mexico that his attitude bordered on sheer defiance. Only a month before, he had encountered on the trail none other than Manuel Armijo, the former governor of New Mexico. Armijo and his escorts were fleeing southward into the heartland to answer charges of cowardice by Mexican officials. The Englishman told Armijo point-blank that he thought the governor and his bunch were "a pack of arrant cowards." General Armijo, "a mountain of fat," according to Ruxton in *Life in the Far West,* waved his hand and retorted, "Adios! They don't know that I had but seventy-five men to fight three thousand. What could I do?"

Arriving in El Paso after leaving Chihuahua, Ruxton told a Mexican sergeant who had been sent to ask the purpose of his mission "to go to the devil." The *prefecto* (chief of police) later asked him, "Where are you bound?"

"Por Santa Fe y Nuevo Mexico," Ruxton answered.

"No, señor," the *prefecto* responded, "this cannot be permitted: by order of the Governor no one is allowed to go to the north. . . . Your passport and other documents?"

The Englishman then produced one of his credentials, which "at once caused the hat to fly from [the *prefecto*'s] head, and [he made] an offer of himself — his house, and all in it, at my disposal," Ruxton recalled. Such a response for a nomad English soldier of fortune!

And so, despite skirmishes with Indians, passages across cracked lake beds, suspicious *prefectos,* frigid nights, and fodderless deserts, George Frederick Ruxton pressed northward, oblivious to danger and treated by others with the kind of respect accorded a messiah. Noli me tangere — don't touch me — he said; I'm English. And they didn't. He not only became the eyes and ears of British interests in the Southwest, but also served as a mediator between Mexican officials and American traders on the Santa Fe Trail.

By the first part of November Ruxton was following the Rio Grande and entering the region known as Jornada del Muerto — the dead man's journey. A broad, baked, dusty, level table of land stretched before him, flanked on the east by the Sacramento Mountains and punctuated by a sprawling laguna in the middle, which was littered with the dry bones of animals and people. At the Jornado's northern end and close to the Rio Grande, Ruxton encountered the Magoffins, as well as a caravan of traders. They had been languishing there in a small village for close to a month, waiting for Colonel Doniphan and his regiment to arrive from the Navaho lands to provide them an escort to El Paso and Chihuahua.

For Susan it had been another opportunity to practice her patience and absorb the local culture. She stayed at the home of a local family, endured a prolonged fever, learned how to make tortillas, sold bales of Samuel's calico prints to the village women, and prepared to make this her winter home. The heavy summer days had given way to pallid November sunshine, and a biting wind scuttled over the desert floor. As she had on the prairie bound for Santa Fe, she took life a day at a time, even though the fear of impending battles on the trail crept into her dreams.

By the time Ruxton arrived Susan was excited to receive news about the road ahead of her. Ruxton told Samuel about the nervous state of things in Chihuahua and that James Magoffin was on trial there for his life. It seems that the Mexicans had implicated him in the scheme with Armijo to quit Santa Fe peacefully. Fear for James compounded Susan's other fears. She went to her room and prayed for James's welfare. She then prayed for herself and Samuel, and in the darkness she chastised herself for not trusting enough in the will of the Lord. "I have not prayed," she confessed to her diary, "with sufficient fervor to have my weak faith strengthened, my perseverance to find religion increased — to have this 'stony heart taken away and to receive a heart of flesh'."

Meanwhile, Ruxton sojourned nearby, visiting the campsites of the Missouri traders scattered through a grove of cottonwoods near the river. The wagons were drawn together in a square to fend off Mexican or Indian attacks. Tents and makeshift shanties were placed close by, and the Missourians idled, swapped yarns, or cooked over fires. A short distance away, several of them shot at targets placed on the cottonwood trunks.

Near the traders' camp, Ruxton encountered a surveying party of topographical engineers under the command of Lt. James Abert. Abert was attached to the Army of the West and was assigned to map the Southwest. He was as good a representational artist as he was a topographer. His sketches of Santa Fe and its environs were as accurate and provocative as any drawings made before 1890, when the first "serious" eastern artists started arriving. Abert had, of course, been at Bent's Fort with Kearny. He had endured heat, dust, fever, and loneliness like the rest of them, and he had grown weary of the vastness and dryness of the Southwest desert.

Ruxton and Abert hit it off from the start, although the Englishman was repulsed by the disorganization of the American soldiers. Rabble in arms, the Yanks scoffed at discipline and loafed around camp. Suppressing any outward signs of the reactions that his spit-and-polish military upbringing prompted, Ruxton watched incredulously as the men stumbled through camp "ragged and dirty, without uniforms, and dressed as, and how, they pleased. They wandered about, listless and sickly looking, or were sitting in groups playing at cards, and swearing and cursing, even at the officers if they interfered to stop it." Ruxton wrote further, "The American can never be made a soldier; his constitution will not bear the restraint of discipline, neither will his very mistaken notions about liberty allow him to subject himself to its necessary control." Later, however, he was quick to add (after the battles of Brazita and Chihuahua) that the Americans had remarkable fighting ability when called upon.

By the fourteenth of December the traders were ready to roll to Chihuahua, and Abert's party prepared to return north to Santa Fe. Ruxton saddled up and went with Abert, partly for protection from the marauding bands preying on travelers.

Following the Rio Grande under a tepid sun, they encountered in turn Socorro and Albuquerque. Having been raised in a country where eclectic buildings were the norm, Ruxton was appalled by "the most extraordinary and primitive specimens of architecture. . . . The decorations of the interior are equal to the promises held out by the imposing outside." They soon departed from the Rio Grande, and a few days before Christmas, arrived in Santa Fe.

Santa Fe, the town that had lured Stephen Kearny, Susan Magoffin, and Gabe Wiggins, now presented itself to the durable Briton. He was not impressed. He wrote of the land, "fertile, but of limited extent"; of the Americans, "the dirtiest, rowdiest, crew I have ever seen collected together"; of the Pueblos, "the most industrious portion of the population"; of the town itself, "I can compare it to nothing but a dilapidated brick kiln or a prairie dog town. . . ."

"Although I had determined to remain some time in Santa Fe to recruit my animals," he remarked, "I was so disgusted with the filth of the town and the disreputable society a stranger was forced into, that in a very few days I packed my mules and proceeded to the north."

What did he expect? London? Rome? Why had Ruxton so little to say about Santa Fe? Did he feel rebuffed and excluded? Perhaps. Governor Bent had extended no greeting to him. Indeed, he was treated like an average traveler, and this may account for the cold shoulder he gave the city.

In early January 1847, Ruxton led Panchita up into the foothills on the trail to Taos. Alone again, the English dude and explorer headed into the Rockies, soon to fall in among the American mountain men and become one of them.

For Charles Bent, Christmas was never more festive than in Santa Fe, where Mexican and Pueblo traditions mixed with familiar American symbols of the season. Cedar boughs decked the Palace and champagne flowed freely. Some of his guests whacked gaily at a piñata in one of the back rooms. Bright lights glowed throughout the music-filled interior and the little adobe on the plaza declared itself against the huge pewter sky.

But three months into his term Charles Bent, under his crust of geniality, was gut-worried. For several months Santa Fe had been protected by a police force under the command of Sterling Price, which had arrived in October to replace the Army of the West. Artillery had been wheeled into the plaza. Outposts had been created on the roads leading in and out of the city. Sentries walked picket duty around the plaza. By December, Santa Fe was wary of a fomenting revolution.

The revolutionaries were, of course, amateurs, mostly Pueblos with Hispanicized names. Their leaders were seasoned veterans of resistance like Diego Archuleta and Thomas Ortiz. They plotted, stole weapons, organized small guerrilla bands, raided the outposts, and more or less kept Price's forces on edge. Some reports stated that the threat of revolution extended as far north as Taos. Into the winter it was clear that the Pueblos were as outraged by the American yoke as they had been by the Spanish for centuries.

While Bent tried desperately to hold a course of quiet diplomacy, he and Price got wind in mid-December of a specific uprising, upon which they acted swiftly. Several instigators were arrested and detained; several escaped, including the important leaders. Right through Christmas, Bent fretted that some unprovoked and bold attack might shake the city. It didn't. Major Clark's artillery, detained from heading southward to join Doniphan, remained conspicuously throughout the town.

Surrounded by the scent of Christmas wreaths and the drifting Spanish music from the dining room, Bent reflected on the year. Outside Santa Fe, everything seemed normal. His lovely Ignacia was safe at their home in Taos. He missed her, especially now. Doniphan was marching southward to the Mexican border, and he knew that a decisive American victory might help prevent a revolution here. Even little Susan Magoffin was out on the Southwestern desert somewhere, in the midst of the chaos. He hoped she was well. James Magoffin was still in a Chihuahua jail, taking the heat for Kearny's bloodless conquest of the city. Bent drank champagne and toasted his guests.

Three weeks later, just behind Ruxton, Governor Bent was riding to Taos, anxious to see Ignacia and to help quell tensions in the valley. Even though he was traveling with a company of officials, there were those in Santa Fe and Taos who argued that he was needlessly exposing himself to danger. Recent snows had clogged the trail, and up on the cedar slopes, heavy drifts still resisted the steady glare of the sun. On they went, Bent buoyed by hopes for the new year, as the mules and horses plodded through the snow.

10. The Road Taken

On an early morning in July, I said good-bye to Felipe, Chile, and Santa Fe. Swinging my pack onto my back, I began to follow Ruxton's and Bent's route to Taos, which leads up between the Sangre de Cristos and the Jemez Range. Their road was a frozen, tortuous little track meandering through the ancient villages of San Juan and La Canada. Just north of Santa Fe, the chalk-colored, bleak foothills give no hint of the cool, pine-streaked slopes ahead.

Route 283 is usually hellish with traffic, especially in summer. It ascends through the barren foothills past Tesuque and Pojoaque pueblos, whose bingo signs lure pedestrians and motorists. The morning sun makes the hot asphalt and dusty shoulder simmer, and afternoon rains lurk over the Sangres and douse the traveler on his way.

Ruxton and Bent followed the trail as it led back to the Rio Grande and then turned northeast through the foothills, approaching Taos from an accessible canyon route. Their journeys were uneventful. Instead of following their trail exactly, I turned right at Pojoaque Pueblo and took the mountain road, Route 503, the so-called high road to Taos. I had planned this diversion beforehand. For one reason, the traffic on the direct route was relentless, the scenery bland. The trail through the Sangres, however, was peaceful, and it included interesting mountain villages and some arresting mountainscapes.

So I let Bent and Ruxton tramp through the snows along the Rio Grande, and I headed up into the mountains. I was not sorry for it. A series of hairpin turns eventually led into the high towns of Cundiyo and Cordova, where goats stood on the street corners and hills swept away on either side. The valleys below were painted in deep summer green. The road through the towns snaked between little churches with their proud white crosses and backyard gardens tall with corn and beans.

There is a wonderful solemnity and serenity in these hidden mountain villages. They have a Peruvian remoteness, tottering on the hilly ridges and surveying the distant canyons beyond. The people, too, seem different, exiles from another time. Seen standing by the road, their faces as tanned and dry as the leather belts they wear over their shoulders, they look wary and suspicious of intruders. But this suspicion is part of the charm of such places. Somehow a forced smile or an extended hand would have been a reminder that I was a tourist — and how badly I wished to pass by unnoticed, to dissolve into the crowd, to be a resident. As I went through the streets, I could only guess how many unsung artists, potters, weavers, furniture makers, and artisans lived on these hillsides.

Were these the mountains that a fugitive named Gabe Wiggins had stumbled into? Had he turned his back on his prairie life and taken up, like George Ruxton, the rugged routine of a mountain man? Had he spent five, ten, or twenty years as an outlaw from society among this dying breed of men?

Unusually humid days persisted. The sun came up over the dark green ridge of the Sangres only to be clouded over by noon. When the rains came, they dropped in furious downpours. One afternoon outside Truchas, I got caught in one. I spent the better part of an hour under the eave of a corrugated steel shed by the side of the road. Thunder boomed and the rain coursed down the pavement in front of me. Nothing moved but the diagonal white sheet of rain.

As the rain subsided I looked up to see a strange sight. Trotting down the strip of asphalt was a collection of farm animals obviously spooked by the storm: several horses, a goat, three dogs, chickens, a burro, and few sheep bringing up the rear. They made right for the center of town, braying, barking, and cackling. A few moments later, an excited farmer came chasing after them, muttering in Spanish and trying to corral them with abrupt gestures. The man did his best to encourage the goat back to the fold, while the chickens strutted off in the other direction.

The rain had stopped completely now, so I followed this mountain roundup into town. By the time I caught up with the group, the animals had snarled traffic and prompted some curious laughs from several townspeople. Soon several of the man's neighbors joined his effort, while a line of cars waited patiently for the road to be cleared. When most of the animals had been corraled, the men focused on the burro, who stood defiantly in the middle of the road and brayed at the cars and men. Wiggling his ears in delight at this new attention, the burro refused all attempts to lure him into joining the other animals. Finally one of the men was able to approach him and smacked him gently on the rear. The burro bolted past the audience at the roadside and headed home.

About midway between Santa Fe and Taos lies Las Trampas, and I arrived there around noon the following day. It was a hot day by Sangre de Cristo standards, about 80 degrees, and so far rainless. The town appeared abandoned, and as I reached the northern end I found out why. Nearly everyone had gathered on the grounds of the 230-year-old José de Gracia Church. They were "remudding" the church walls, an event that takes place every other year or so and includes the entire community.

The best mud, or adobe, is a combination of sand, clay, water, and silt. Chopped straw is mixed in as a fixative so that the adobe will not crack in the sum. No other ingredients need be added. When wet, adobe is extremely pliable; when dry, it is hard, durable, and nearly waterproof. Especially in the New Mexican climate, where the sun can be torrid, the walls of adobe buildings efficiently absorb heat during the day and release it into the interior at night. Most importantly, perhaps, adobe houses and churches don't creak, rattle, or tremble in any weather. Their dried walls are stone hard, supporting a firmly rooted structure and creating a sanctuary of silence inside. Add the diffused interior light and you have an ideal marriage of form and function.

It was easy to sense the community pride that ruled the "mudding" of the church that day. Each person had a specific role and worked enthusiastically. When I walked up, the men of the village were digging dirt and, with the help of children and teenagers, were mixing it with water and straw in the back of an old Ford pickup. The women were talking and planning their sculpting strategies — the application and sculpting of the wet adobe is traditionally the women's role.

Once a good supply of mud had been made, the women climbed the scaffolding that had been erected and slapped the buttery goo on the walls, smoothing it carefully with trowels. Sometimes they hand-smoothed the mud or used a wet sheepskin.

They chattered and looked at the sky, hoping it wouldn't rain. Occasionally an overseer passed under the scaffold, examining the women's work and offering some casual tips in Spanish. "Those drips won't get you into heaven," he chuckled to one woman. Everyone was occupied by a task of some kind, but the work was spiced with humor and tomfoolery. The scene soon resembled one of those Brueghel paintings in which hosts of villagers busy themselves around a church or tavern, all the while gossiping, eating, and laughing.

The day lengthened, but the rain did not come. One woman in her sixties standing on the scaffold pointed to the blue, barren sky with a mud-splattered hand. She laughed and crossed herself. The other women smiled and nodded. The afternoon sun would bake dry the newly mudded section. And like the fresco painters of the Renaissance, the townspeople of Las Trampas would return again the next day and proceed with the project. Perhaps it wouldn't rain tomorrow either and they could make more headway, I said. "If it rains, it rains," a woman replied. "We'll do something else tomorrow. We'll come back the day after, or the day after that. Soon the sun will shine for a long time. Then we can finish."

I returned to the road that runs northeast, then at Penasco jogs due east and meets Route 3, which approaches Taos from the south. I camped at Tierra Azul, where I spent half the night copying some of the illegible scrawls from Gabe Wiggins's journal, hoping to achieve clarity. A warm dry wind blew down from the Sangres, bearing with it the pungent scent of cedar and pine. The next morning I strapped on my pack and headed the short distance to Taos.

Late in 1846 George Ruxton was entering the region and beginning to discover just how deep local animosities ran toward the conquering Americans.

Urging Panchita through the deep snows, he came to the home of an Indian family who offered him a meal and a place to stay. Realizing he was English and not American, the mother exclaimed,

"Gracias a Dios! A Christian will sleep with us tonight and not an American!"

Ruxton ate with them and joined fourteen other people bedded down on the floor. Several chickens cackled around him as he drifted to sleep. But this humble shelter was better than the frigid slopes of the Sangres!

On the seventeenth of January, 1847, Charles Bent was approaching the outskirts of Taos. He was glad he had refused a military escort. What message would that have sent to his friends in the valley? In many ways, he felt, he was coming home. Ever since he had moved into his little adobe north of the plaza in the mid-1830s, Taos had been his spiritual roost. Besides, Ignacia was there, and over the years they had developed friendships with local families. The town felt comfortable to him — a place to stretch his legs and relax from the cares of life. So he was going home. Just for a few days, he wanted to forget the pressures of his job and the instability of Santa Fe.

Unfortunately, no one had told the Pueblos.

11. The Valley in Turmoil

For centuries Taos Pueblo has huddled under a mountain's rim, a peaceful island in a tumultuous sagebrush sea. It is small and compact by the Pueblo Indians' building standards, but it has a majestic presence as it surveys the valley sloping to the Rio Grande. Before there was a village or plaza in Taos, there were the mountain, the pueblo, and the valley, terraced stepping stones for the gods to descend from the sacred peaks.

Surmounting the pueblo is Pueblo Peak, which dominates the surrounding meadows and influences the beliefs of the Pueblo Indians. Pueblo Peak has always been sacred, ever since the Ancient Ones emerged from the dank underworld in its core and suffered much on their way to the earth's light. Lost children, called kachinas, guided them as they crept out of the underworld, moved down into villages, and cultivated the land. The Pueblos worship mountains and mesas as the source of life. Even today, kachinas have been known to travel down from the mountain and join in the festive and sacred dances at Taos Pueblo. And so in the shadow of the peak, the Pueblos developed an elaborate system of myths that explained death and birth, sowing and harvesting, and war and peace.

When the Spanish entered the valley in the sixteenth century, they immediately began upsetting traditional Pueblo beliefs by introducing Christianity. The Pueblos, however, weaned on the idea of a multitude of gods, rejected the Spanish-Catholic notions of baptism, self-torture, punishable sin, and a personal God. For a hundred years, although the Pueblo and Spanish cultures merged in some areas, they grew decisively apart in others. The Spanish ultimately feared Pueblo mysticism and the peyote cult; the Pueblos despised their oppressors for trying to shape Pueblo religion into a form of Christianity.

By the 1670s tensions had increased and hostilities had reached a flash point, as the Spanish had begun arresting and killing village priests for sorcery and witchcraft. The aggrieved Pueblos revolted in 1680 at Taos, and by the time the week-long bloodbath was over, close to 350 Indians and Spanish lay dead or wounded in the fields. The revolt symbolized the lingering Pueblo fear of suffocation by outsiders, and all Pueblos from that day forward carried the idea that not only could they resist tyranny, they could also take action against it.

By the beginning of the 1820s the Spanish no longer ruled the territory, and the little village of San Fernandez de Taos had mushroomed about a mile south of the pueblo. The two camps kept their distance. The Pueblos carried on their centuries-old rituals in secrecy; the Spaniards in the town crowded into the single-room adobes and developed a sluggish trade with Santa Fe. Interlopers began filtering through: Americans, mainly trappers and fur traders, who started to use San Fernandez as one of the southern headquarters of the beaver trade. The Americans also brewed Taos lightning, which over the years appeased and later corrupted the Pueblos.

In the next few years the Taos valley became a capital of Yankee commerce. It soon resembled one of the great northern trappers' rendezvous, but this one had a distinctly southern flair: French explorers and entrepreneurs traveled down from the north looking for contraband and Indian slaves; Navahos from the west brought blankets and turquoise; Mexicans from Chihuahua came in wagons laden with gaudy textiles and gourds of wine; Comanches leading strings of stolen horses rode through and joined the throngs of howling and bartering traders mingling amid the deep summer grasses.

Into this rowdy bazaar rode twenty-four-year-old Ceran St. Vrain. In the mid-1820s St. Vrain thought that Taos was one of the great commercial secrets of the Southwest. He was good-natured, dark-haired, built like a blockhouse, and very ambitious. He came from Bent's Fort to Taos determined to make something of the place. Despite its squalor, its dusty remoteness, and its gypsum-coated adobes, St. Vrain liked the town. Perhaps it was his French-Catholic background or the swarms of men gossiping and smoking cornhusk cigarettes that made him feel welcome. Or maybe it was that indescribable quality that artists and writers have been trying to evoke for most of the twentieth century.

Whatever it was, St. Vrain soon exploited it. He accepted some of the town's evils as part of the cost of doing business. Gambling was rampant and snared men and women alike. Justice could be quick or nonexistent, depending on the reputation of the person involved. Profanity was everywhere, and morals were loose. On the other hand, there were local customs that St. Vrain truly enjoyed. "Fandangos," for instance, occasioned some grand and festive gatherings of villagers. They could be held in the open air or in the *sala* (parlor) of a local adobe, and they drew traders, businessmen, and young women whose twirling bodies shone with turquoise bracelets, earrings, necklaces, and weighty silver crosses.

Besides burrowing into the Taos culture, St. Vrain encouraged trade with Missouri and developed an operation to outfit the Rocky Mountain trapper. He did all three well, and by the time he had begun a business partnership with Charles Bent around 1830, he had made Taos a wealthy mountain village.

Bent left the Taos trade nearly exclusively to St. Vrain. However, he journeyed there several times to monitor operations. Bent, St. Vrain and Co. soon opened an outlet on the south side of Taos's plaza. Charles, like his partner Ceran, soon came to regard the town as a rowdy but secluded terminus on the trail to the Southwest. He began calling himself Carlos Bent and married Ignacia, daughter of a prominent New Mexican family. They came to Taos as a couple in 1836 and set up housekeeping in a rambling adobe close to the firm's store. There were trips, of course, to Bent's Fort to attend to business matters and confer with brother William. But as the 1840s approached, Charles Bent viewed Taos as home and began spreading down roots to reaffirm this commitment.

As for the Pueblos during this time, they could be controlled but not suppressed. Another violent Pueblo revolt in 1837 proved that. They continued to use a few Christian principles in their lives and conveniently discarded the rest. Mexican padres chiseled away at this stony resistance and won some converts. Along the way, they warned the Pueblos of increasing American interests in the region; this, of course, was unsettling news.

One of the padres, Antonio Martinez, maintained a particular dislike of Americans in general and Charles Bent specifically. The grudge between the two was old and bitter. Martinez had returned to Taos in 1826 after taking his vows in Durango and began winning over the Pueblos and Mexican citizens. He could speak eloquently about the wonders of Catholicism; he could also, when talking to the Pueblos, declare that the kachinas were the most beautiful beings on earth. He quickly abandoned celibacy in Taos, reasoning that if he was to understand the nature of sin, he had to lower himself into it. Martinez also spurned Bent and St. Vrain's attempts to capitalize on the merits of little Taos. He wooed the leaders of the Taos Pueblo, siding with them in the 1837 uprising. At every turn, he blocked Bent's endeavors to get close to the townspeople. Bent in his turn viewed Padre Martinez as a scoundrel and tyrant, who was nothing more than a hotspur igniting Pueblo suspicions. The feud continued right into 1846, with tempers running high and nervous fears keeping things on edge.

By the time Kearny had arrived in Santa Fe and installed Charles Bent as governor, an unspoken Mexican-Pueblo alliance had begun to emerge up and down the Rio Grande. As American influence spread, tensions and hatreds grew like wildfire. The Mexican-Pueblo enclave in Taos drew closer and went underground, joining other bands in Santa Fe and elsewhere in hitting vulnerable American targets. As 1847 began, Charles Bent appeared to be the embodiment of American imperialism in New Mexico.

The Pueblos never forgot Spanish rule or the years 1680 and 1837. The Mexicans and Padre Martinez helped remind them.

On the evening of January 18, 1847, Charles Bent puttered around his Taos adobe and chatted with his family, occasionally stirring the piñon logs in the fireplace. Before going to bed, he made sure the house was secure. There had been some disturbances in the town, although they were no cause for general alarm. He heard some random shouts and gunfire outside, but he thought it was some drunk that Sheriff Steve Lee would soon cart off to jail. He went to his room and climbed into bed.

Taos seemed all right. The Pueblos were somewhat agitated — something about wanting several of their comrades released from jail. But it appeared that the arrival of Bent had temporarily appeased them. George Ruxton had passed through town a few days before and stayed with Sheriff Lee. Wishing to press on to the Colorado Rockies, Ruxton left hastily, avoiding a measles epidemic that had recently broken out in the valley. The nearby Bent–St.

Vrain ranch was quiet. A prairie sourdough named Louie Symonds was bunking there, soon to return to his haunts around Bent's Fort. Aside from the usual punctuation of shots and voices, Taos remained calm, drifting into a cold sleep.

A sliver of moon rose, and the chill deepened in the dark of early morning. Across town, the light in Pablo Montoya's adobe flickered and then steadied. Near the bright little flame, he leaned over the pine table, looking intensely at a list of names he had scribbled. All night long he had been sending out couriers to Taos Pueblo, hoping to finalize the elements of his plan. Horsemen were arriving outside. Muskets were rattling and mounts were neighing in the dark. Several of the Pueblo riders came in, their dark hair pulled back in warrior fashion. They were loud now, full of venom.

They drained flasks of Taos lightning and listened to Montoya's diatribes. Berserk with liquor and their own wild fears, they hooted and chanted. They knew this was it — that this day Pueblo honor would be fully realized. Charles Bent had come to them, played right into their hands.

Montoya and his men drank the last of the liquor and moved out, bearing Montoya's list of Americans to call on. Among them were Circuit Attorney James Leal, Prefect Cornelio Vigil, Sheriff Steve Lee, and the governor himself. Where was Padre Martinez? He was not with the conspirators at dawn, though Ceran St. Vrain later believed that he was the catalyst of the morning's tragedy.

Charles Bent awoke around seven to the sound of footsteps outside and muffled voices in the courtyard. He bolted up and dressed hurriedly. Rubbing the sleep from his eyes, he called through the door, "What do you want?" His heart was throbbing, his voice dry. There a came a confused answer: many voices muttering in Spanish.

He glanced behind him. Ignacia was up, and terror was in her eyes. She handed out his pistols to him, but he refused them because they might inflame the situation. Instead, he moved back into the rear of the house and told Ignacia to begin digging through the wall into the adjoining house. He herded his frightened children toward her as she began tearing and gouging the thick adobe wall with a fire poker.

Bent gulped and tried to prepare a diplomatic defense. The attackers were beating at the door. He shouted, offering them money. They hooted him down and continued to ram the door. As more ideas flooded his brain, he heard footsteps running above him. My God! A hammer was clawing through the roof! He leaned toward the door again and offered himself as a prisoner, hoping to spare his family and the other Americans in Taos. More wails rose outside, and musket butts began splintering the door.

Ignacia and the children had opened a hole in the wall and had begun worming through it. A hail of musket balls riddled the door, and several pierced it. Bent clutched his stomach and fell. More musket butts tore through the door, and arrows flew through an opening, hitting both the floor and the prone figure. Bent rallied briefly. Pulling arrows from his chest, he struggled to the rear of the house and stood dazed in the front of the hole in the wall. He almost made it through the breach.

Weakness felled him. Bleeding and in shock, he dropped to his knees. Pueblos broke through the door. Others dropped from a gaping hole in the ceiling. Bent fell on his chest as the warriors surged toward him. They danced over his fallen figure. One of the Pueblos leaned over and scalped him with a bowstring. Life drained from him. Ignacia and the children were safe, he thought, and then he thought . . . nothing.

The attackers chanted and howled over the body until one of them cried out that they had murdered their most valuable hostage. They stopped dancing, staring at Bent's lifeless figure and shifting dubiously around it. One screamed, grabbed Bent's scalp, and with the others following, raced out into the street. They charged through the town, brandishing Bent's gray hair.

Charles Bent lay dead in a pool of blood beside the crude hole in the wall. Dead too, across town, were Cornelio Vigil and Steve Lee. James Leal's death was crueler — he was shot and then scalped while he was still conscious.

By nine in the morning, the American stores in Taos had already been looted. It was quiet, save for the cries of the families. Smoke curled from a number of blackened stores. Riders leaped on horses, so bewildered by the nightmare that they raced for Santa Fe by heading north.

Taos was in shock. There were those, too, who grabbed a noose in one hand and a musket in the other.

12. Resolution

The next day Pablo Montoya fled into the mountains and organized a haughty bunch of rebels into a rag-tag guerrilla band. They had killed a governor, a sheriff, and an attorney and had ransacked their own village. Bolstered by their quick victory, the insurgents felt confident that they could spread their revolution south to Santa Fe.

Hearing the frantic news from town, Louie Symonds quickly left the Bents' ranch and headed for Bent's Fort by way of Raton Pass. All of a sudden it seemed that Taos — no, the entire Southwest — was in turmoil, and he hastened to spread the tragic news. He knew that if Taos and Santa Fe were taken, Bent's Fort would be the revolutionaries' next target. He was not alone in his errand; other messengers were hurrying in different directions.

With the Taos outrage still fresh, Symonds reminded himself as he traveled of his most urgent mission: to find William Bent and tell him what happened to his brother. He urged his horse through the snowy New Mexican meadows, heading northeast, then scaled Raton Pass and came down into the Purgatoire valley. The grizzled Symonds, his tawny mustache cascading over his lips, watched for armed Mexicans along the river bank as he rode along. Forty miles south of the fort, following a row of cottonwoods, he encountered a cluster of Cheyenne tepees and log houses on either side of the Purgatoire River. In one of those log houses, young Lewis Garrard of Cincinnati was squatting with his traveling buddy, John Smith, and trading beads for meat with an old Indian woman. Garrard had been in the vicinity of Bent's Fort for nearly three months, dividing his time between the fort and the Cheyenne villages around it. Other traders were with him, scattered throughout the camp.

Symonds burst into the village, relating the news from Taos. He was surrounded immediately by a host of angry traders and mountain men in various guises. William Bent was among them.

"'Scalped him! Scalped Charles?' cried the men, reaching for their long knives. 'Thar be a heap of wolf meat afore long, sartain,'" Garrard wrote later in *Wah-to-Yah and the Taos Trail.*

As the men stammered and spat, Symonds told them about Charles and the others, including as much wild rumor and embroidered truth as the moment called for.

"'Will they take Santy Fee, think ye, Louie?'" one of them asked.

"'Now,'" said Symonds, "that's more than this hoss kin tell. He hasn't made medicine yet; but I'm afraid the 'Mericans will 'go under'."

As alarm turned into anger around the camp, young Garrard watched William Bent take Symonds aside and interrogate him about Charles's death. Desire for vengeance raged in William. He sent Louie away and grabbed Garrard; together they rode back to Bent's Fort to make preparations for a raid on Taos.

A grim William Bent said nothing as they journeyed across the prairie, and Garrard held his tongue. They encountered a lone Mexican on the trail, and Bent nearly shot him out of pure rage. Up the river lay the fort and a company of men and parties of Cheyennes who would soon hear of the Taos massacre. Bent would make certain that their reprisal would be quick and violent. In *Wah-to-Yah and the Taos Trail* Garrard reported his orders: "Kill and scalp every Mexican to be found, and collect all the animals belonging to the Company and the United States."

This trip was turning into an exciting adventure after all, thought Lewis Garrard.

From the time he was very young in Ohio, Lewis Hector Garrard was in love with the mystique of the West, with mountain and prairie lore. Like Francis Parkman, he was enamored of Cooper's and Irving's vivid depictions of it. In spring 1846, fed up with merely reading about it, he tossed aside his books, packed his bags, journeyed to St. Louis and Westport, and prepared to travel overland on the Santa Fe Trail. He craved romance and danger, especially the western brand with its fierce Comanches, towering peaks, and hardy mountain men.

Barely seventeen, Garrard was fortunate to travel to Bent's Fort that autumn in the company of Ceran St. Vrain. The robust

St. Vrain provided him with a smooth transition between civilization and the raw trail (Garrard later dedicated his book *Wah-to-Yah and the Taos Trail* to St. Vrain). Through September and October they traveled west to Colorado, St. Vrain acting as interpreter and mentor for the young Garrard. They arrived at Bent's Fort in November, and there Garrard met William Bent. Later he was introduced to a collection of mountain men and wanderers who called the fort home: John Smith, the St. Louis–born trader who spent his entire life among the Cheyennes; Louie Symonds, the gravel-voiced scout and hunter who knew the eastern Sangre de Cristos better than anyone at the fort; and John Hatcher, the flinty frontier mercenary who was full of tall tales.

Toward the beginning of February 1847, Garrard and twenty-two other men left Bent's Fort, heading southwest on the Santa Fe Trail to avenge Charles Bent's murder. William Bent remained at the fort. Perhaps he had been talked out of going because a personal vendetta on his part might upset the expedition. It was almost six months to the day since Stephen Kearny had led his cavalcade in the same direction. But it was midwinter now, and the sun was no enemy but a friend, melting some of the waist-deep drifts of snow that had piled up along the trail.

Among the group was a contingent of Canadian voyageurs, whose rollicking humor provided the company with some much-needed levity. While most of the Americans rode to Taos on horseback, the Canadians walked and seemed not at all bothered by the arduous trek. They chatted in French, commenting on the surrounding landscape, and tested their sharpshooting skills on anything and everything. If one of them stopped to aim at a distant target, the rest would stand on tiptoe with open mouths, waiting expectantly for the flash and loud crack of the gun. Then they would hurry over to the target and inspect it, while someone exclaimed "Sacrebleu!" over his shoulder. At night before the fire, the Canadians sat in circles talking with their American comrades, short clay pipes dangling from their hairy lips.

They crossed the same barren stretch of ground leading to the Purgatoire River that Kearny, Gabe Wiggins, and the Magoffins had, each in turn, feared, cursed, and loathed. Most of the greasewood and sagebrush that dotted the sand had been uprooted by Kearny's army for firewood. But there was still beauty to be seen on the journey in the snow-streaked profiles of the Spanish Peaks, which rose over the blanched winter prairie. Garrard smiled — he was at last seeing the landmarks promised him by Cooper and Irving and a score of mountain men at Bent's Fort. Below them, however, from one horizon to the other, the wind blew unimpeded in the bleak Timpas valley, bringing in quick snow squalls that slowed the little company.

They kept on. The Canadians smoked, shot, and chattered. Dressed in his wool hat and heavy wool "hickory" shirt, Garrard nodded along on his mount watching the Spanish Peaks fade from sight. Some of the Taoseños in the group fretted about their families' welfare. But when they came to the cottonwoods and the loamy banks of the Purgatoire, their thoughts turned to crossing Raton Pass and facing enemy bands on the other side.

Having no wagons or artillery to bog them down, they threaded up Raton's steep passageways, even though some fierce winter drifts clogged the trail. Then New Mexico spread before them. The Santa Fe Trail veered to the southwest, and forking to the right from it was the Taos Trail, which led up through the mountains.

On the other side of the pass they encountered one of Bent's Indians riding from the south. His name was Haw-he, and he bore good news: the Americans under Colonel Price and Ceran St. Vrain out of Santa Fe had recently smashed a Mexican-Pueblo army near Taos. Many Mexicans and Pueblos had been killed and several prisoners taken. The Taos Pueblo was under the American flag. The group from Bent's Fort would not have to fight after all.

It was mid-February when Garrard and company crossed the Cimarron River and turned up into the high country, following the Taos Trail.

During the first week of April the Taos courtroom was conspicuously cold, even though the young spring sun squeezed through two narrow windows and fell in thin shafts on the floor. Rats scurried between the benches, around the piles of oak shavings and ridges of dirt in their way. The ceilings were high and the air smelled dusty and stale. Rows of crude benches filled the oblong interior, separated from the witness stands by a slender rail. A bench for the witnesses clung to the wall. Flies droned in the silence.

Just before nine in the morning, Garrard, John Hatcher, Louie Symonds, and some of the Canadians took off their wool hats and filed into the courtroom. The room soon swelled with activity, with the scrape of boots on the oak flooring and the sound of muffled coughs and voices as people entered and sat down.

The presiding judges were Joab Houghton, a friend of Charles Bent's, and Carlos Beaubien, whose son had been among the slain in Taos. Charles and William's brother George was foreman of the grand jury, and the rest of the jury consisted mostly of Bent's cronies. Ceran St. Vrain was there to serve as interpreter. The prosecuting attorney was Frank Blair, barely twenty-two years old and out to draw quick blood.

Six prisoners were to be tried in the first session. Nine more would be dealt with in a few days. The two principal leaders of the uprising, Romero and Montoya, were both dead — Romero had been shot by a young army recruit, and Montoya had been captured and executed by Price's forces when they entered Taos.

Beaubien and Houghton stared grimly around the courtroom. An invocation was read, and Beaubien called the court to order. The six prisoners were led in, "ill-favored, half-scared, sullen fellows," wrote Garrard later.

Frank Blair strode forward and read the charges: five murder counts and one treason. "Treason, indeed!" mused Garrard. "What did the poor devil know about his allegiance?"

Several Mexican witnesses were called. They came up as "frightened as the prisoners at the bar," observed Garrard; kissed the Bible; took their oaths; and sat down. Blair fired point-blank questions at them, and St. Vrain added some dramatic inflections to the translation. The witnesses answered as best they could. The members of the jury sat intently, dwelling on each word of testimony.

Blair finally sat down. Beaubien gave instructions to the jury and dismissed them. A few minutes later they filed back in and offered their verdict: guilty in the first degree. No one was really surprised, but at least it helped settle several months' turmoil.

Because the jail was crowded, Carlos Beaubien moved up the execution to the following Friday — April ninth. Garrard looked sympathetically at the row of condemned men as the observers rose and shuffled out.

A few days later, nine more prisoners were led into the dock while Garrard, Hatcher, and Symonds sat impassively in the gallery. On a bench against the wall near the judges sat Ignacia Bent, Josefa Carson (Kit's wife), and a friend of the Bents, Rumalda Boggs. Ignacia sat solemnly, her hands folded on her lap. She was not yet thirty years old; her luxuriant raven hair cascaded over her black-draped shoulders. She stared straight ahead, only briefly distracted by the movements of Frank Blair and the fidgetings of the row of prisoners across from her.

Blair stood up and called Ignacia to the stand. She went up, kissed the Bible, and took the oath. Clutching her handkerchief, she recounted the events of the morning of January nineteenth: how Charles Bent arose and encountered the berserk mob at their door ... how she hacked her way through the wall to the adjoining house ... how her husband pleaded with the attackers for his life ... how he refused his pistols ... how he died valiantly just before he could have escaped through the hole ... how they scalped him ... and so on.

Frank Blair asked Ignacia if her husband's killer was in the courtroom. She nodded and pointed to a Pueblo chief sitting with the other prisoners. His face emotionless and his lips sealed, the chief stared back at Ignacia without moving a muscle. She looked away, and then stepped down.

On execution day Garrard, Hatcher, Symonds, and the Canadians awoke to a cloudless spring morning and watched the sun creep over Taos Mountain. It was dead silent. A donkey brayed in the distance. A woman poked her head out of one of the adobes, stared, adjusted her shawl, and withdrew.

Lacking stout lariats, the sheriff borrowed Garrard's and Hatcher's and soaped them till they were pliable. In *Wah-to-Yah and the Taos Trail,* Garrard described the scene this way: "'This'll make 'em slip easy,' explained Metcalf. 'A long ways too easy for them, I 'spect.'" He later charged the U.S. government twelve and a half cents for "greasing nooses."

By nine o'clock the sun was flooding the sandy patch of soil where the execution was to take place. The condemned prisoners waited silently in the Taos jail, "ragged, lousy, greasy, unwashed," observed Garrard. The padres filed out of the jail and solemnly passed the guards.

Soldiers marched onto the grounds and formed three sides of a square. Garrard, Hatcher, and the rest of the mountaineers formed the fourth side. Standing in their leathers and soiled wool hats, they were a ragtag contrast to the disciplined formation of the soldiers.

Garrard saw the prisoners coming. Hatcher took a plug of tobacco and worked it into the corner of his mouth. Symonds stared at the accused as they shuffled past, his caplock resting securely in the crook of his arm. A hush came over the spectators gathered on the rooftops overlooking the square.

In front of Garrard a government wagon pulled by two mules waited under a crossbeam. A single board was balanced across the rear of the wagon. The soldiers led the six prisoners one by one up and along the board. Balanced precariously on the plank with nooses around their necks, the prisoners muttered departing words to the townspeople. As the hood was pulled over his face, one snarled, "Caraho, los Americanos!"

The sheriff gave the word. The mules were lashed and they bolted forward, leaving the six bodies dangling and twisting from the crossbeam. One of the dying men grabbed his neighbor's hand and held on till his grip finally loosened. The bodies swung there for forty minutes. Then Garrard and his companions helped the sheriff untie the nooses and take the bodies down. As they began to cut the rope from one man's neck, Garrard recounts that the driver of the death wagon snapped, "'Hello, there! Don't cut that rope! I won't have anything to tie my mules with.'

"'You darned fool,' retorted a mountaineer, 'the palous [palace] ghosts'll be after you if you use them 'riatas [lariats] — wagh! They'll make meat of you, sartain.'

"'Well I don't care if they do,' [the driver replied]. 'I'm in government service . . . an' money's scarce in these diggins, and I'm gwine to save all I kin.'"

The ropes were tucked away for future use, and the men headed down to Estes's tavern to sample the local eggnog and celebrate the occasion.

They drank and danced, and Lewis Garrard half forgot that they had executed six men that day to avenge Bent's murder and temporarily subdued a revolution in New Mexico.

13. The View From Here

Although the art galleries have replaced Estes's Tavern on today's Kit Carson Road, modern Taos still remembers John Hatcher, Lewis Garrard, George Ruxton, and Charles Bent through the preservation of its nineteenth-century heritage. And even though the town center is often jammed with tourists, Taos still has the leather-and-cornhusk smell, the bearded and flinty look of a nineteenth-century western village. Despite its superficial boutiques and souvenir dens, it still bears the stamp of a genuine article. It will never grow up and behave itself. Good.

Around ten in the morning, just before I was to meet Paul, I walked through the plaza and stood in front of Charles Bent's adobe, which is now a museum. I hung around for several minutes, thinking of the events of that January morning in 1847. Hardly anybody was stirring. The place seemed so damned innocuous and lonely as it squatted on the other side of the street in the hot sun. Three or four parking meters stood on the curb in front; somebody must have rammed one with his car, because the meter leaned, oddly askew, toward the door. In my mind I replayed the events of Charles Bent's murder, freeze-framing some of the dramatic moments and adding some howls and cries. Satisfied with my creative efforts, I turned and strolled back to my hotel.

Paul showed up about ten minutes late, clean-shaven, grinning, and wearing a ready-for-bear look. As we drove to our point of departure I briefed him on the trip. We hoisted up our packs and headed north on State Route 522, which eventually leads to the Colorado border. We had a swift pace going by the time Taos Pueblo appeared on our right. Paul reached in his pocket, brought out his pipe, and lit it without breaking stride. As we hiked along I asked Paul what had been happening at home. His report was brief: nothing. When I travel I tend to imagine that empires are falling during my absence. It was a relief in a way to know that the world, my world, had followed its inevitable course without me.

A couple of days later we got to the rendezvous, which was held in a large clearing in the mountains due north of Taos Pueblo. Aspen and cedar surrounded us, and the clear sun poured onto the meadow, where a collection of tents, lean-tos, and tepees sprouted from the grass. Paul had brought a primitive lean-to, which we set up in a wooded corner of the clearing. There was a fire pit nearby, and before long we had settled into a mountain man existence along with the other people who now congregated in the meadow. I guessed there were between fifty and seventy-five camps dotting the clearing; many contained whole families.

Toward midday, knots of riflemen in deerskins appeared in the center of the meadow. Their leggins had beads sewn up the sides in differing patterns that represented various Indian tribes. Some wore coonskin caps; others were bareheaded. They cradled — very carefully, I might add — heavy muzzle-loaders, including the trappers' favorite, the Hawken caplock. The shooting events were to begin shortly, so there was much excitement around camp.

Paul was in his element. He mingled with the mountain men, asking them about their regalia. Soon he was swapping stories with them. I think he could have adopted this way of life on the spot, for he laughed with the kind of robust ardor that people usually save for holidays and special occasions. He took one of the men's caplocks in hand, felt its weight, scanned its stock and bore carefully, and aimed it at an imaginary target near the trees.

Everything had the look of a trapper's camp in the 1840s — the people, the outfits, the weapons, the lingo. As I surveyed the scene I realized that these were the heirs of the men whom Ruxton, Garrard, and Parkman had so carefully observed over a century and a half ago. These were Hatcher's and Symonds's successors; Ceran St. Vrain's, Kit Carson's, and Henry Chatillon's. Ultimately it is the mountain man who should stand as the symbol of the resourcefulness, independence, and courage of the settlers of the West.

As we talked with various parties of men and women, one of the leaders, a man named Evans, hailed us.

"You're greenhorns out of Taos, eh?" he grinned. "C'mon, and I'll show you around."

Evans's given name (a mountain man usually has a name given him by his comrades or by Indians) was Owl Eyes because of the way he opened his eyes wide when talking. He wore a hat made of coyote skin, and blue and white Crow beads adorned the side of his leggins. He showed us the assortment of events on the schedule and introduced us to many people throughout camp. They came from all over. There we met Powder Horn and Chrome Dome from Colorado and Montana; Squinty and Feather Head from Arizona and Utah; Badger and Dog Soldier from southern New Mexico. They were all bartering and bantering, throwing out tales that, like clay pigeons, others quickly shot down.

Despite their grittiness, they were the politest group of people I've ever met, and very conscious of the strict rules that governed their get-togethers. They seemed to respect themselves and those they emulated. Yet they knew the limits of earnest conversation and refused to take themselves too seriously. They also had an infectious camaraderie. Some were lawyers and accountants, others bricklayers and toolmakers. One was a priest (although in his Arapaho beads he seemed far from the cloister). Here in this meadow, they were all equals — except at the shooting events, where they vied fiercely for superiority.

Paul and I stayed in camp for two days, taking part in several events and cooking over an open fire. On the second afternoon Paul had competed in the so-called "mountain man run," which consisted of loading and shooting a caplock from a horse, throwing a tomahawk, and setting a trap. He had come in last, but it didn't dim his competitive spirit.

After our dinner of scrambled eggs and bacon we collected the mess tins and put them by the lean-to. Over the meadow other fires were going. Night fell softly as the smoke from the blazes drifted through the grass and lifted into the trees. A sudden coolness arose from the forest, and as darkness deepened a silence reigned, so that the others' voices became distant whispers, and we were left with the solitude of our own corner of the universe.

Paul got up and hobbled into the lean-to. Returning, he added more wood to the fire. It blazed momentarily, sending up sparks that died quickly in the night. I sipped tea from a battered tin cup and stretched my legs toward the flames.

Rummaging through a bag, Paul brought out two pipes and offered one to me, saying, "Here. I always keep a couple extra."

He handed me some tobacco and we went through the ceremony that pipe smokers look forward to: the stuffing of the bowl, the lighting of the tobacco, the sucking on the stem, the sighting of that first burst of smoke.

Content, Paul leaned back and yawned. He was curious about my trip to Santa Fe and Taos and the people — historical and modern — I had encountered. He of course remembered Parkman and Bent's Fort and was eager to hear of the rest: Susan Magoffin, Stephen Kearny, Charles Bent, George Ruxton, Lewis Garrard — and Gabe Wiggins. Briefly I filled him in on the mystery surrounding Gabe — Cal and Barbara's place in Trinidad, Gabe's journal, his journey to Santa Fe, the incident there, his disappearance. Paul stroked his chin, perplexed as I was by the whole thing.

I took a sip of tea. "The lives of all these people, except, of course, Gabe Wiggins's, get tied up rather neatly in the end," I told him. "Tragically in some cases, but neatly. I'll come back to Gabe in a moment. As for the others, your friend Francis Parkman went back to Boston and began a career as a historian. He lived to a fairly ripe age. He got to sit at the head of the table, I believe." Paul grinned. "Then Stephen Kearny: he led the Army of the West to California, where he was wounded twice in the battle for San Pasqual, and later became a major general. In 1847 he ended up in Mexico and caught yellow fever. This weakened him, and he died in 1848 in St. Louis, in the home of Maj. Meriwether Lewis Clark. The curious thing about Kearny was that, had he lived, he would have made a fine Civil War general — maybe even a great president. But his greatness rests on that long march from Leavenworth to Santa Fe."

Paul stared briefly at me and muttered, "Hmmm." He puffed his pipe and looked back at the flames. "And the Magoffins?"

"Even more tragic, in some ways," I replied. "James Magoffin — the initial messenger to travel to Santa Fe — bribed his way out of a Chihuahua jail in 1847 and headed for El Paso, where he came under American protection. James settled there. In 1861 he declared for the Confederacy; his son Joseph became the first mayor of El Paso.

"Susan Magoffin was a different story. She and Samuel continued on to Mexico. She too got yellow fever, in Matamoros, and had a son who died shortly after birth. She and her husband returned to the states by sea, settling first in Kentucky, then in Missouri. Susan never recovered from her journey down the trail. She died just short of her thirtieth birthday. It seems sad and ironic that the very country she loved ultimately led to her early death."

I stared silently into the fire — perhaps too long, for Paul said, "I think you admired her."

"Yes, I did. She had moxie, and she had the ability to let go of control, which is one of the first signs that you're ready for the rigors of the prairie. She also had a childlike acceptance of things as they are, without judgment, something Parkman and Ruxton didn't have."

"Speaking of Ruxton," said Paul, "what happened to him?"

"Ruxton seemed to have an amazing gift for avoiding calamity. I mean, he craved adventure and danger — but when there was a real disaster, he was always just ahead of it, or behind it. Take the Taos massacre, for instance: he missed it by a couple of days. He complained that Steve Lee's place didn't have enough pasturage for his animals, so off he went, traveling up to the Colorado Rockies. He could have been killed and scalped like the rest of them. Charles Bent, of course, was in the wrong place at the wrong time. Ruxton wintered around Pikes Peak and lived with the mountain men, absorbing their culture and lingo. By April 1847 he was on his way east and ran into Lewis Garrard near Bent's Fort.

"Garrard seems to have been smitten by Ruxton's worldliness. *Lord* Ruxton, thought Garrard. Ruxton, of course, told the youngster about all his worldwide adventures. Garrard was in awe of him. They went on a wolf hunt together, which Garrard enjoyed. They spent a whole season among drifters and mountain men and were eager to return to civilization afterwards.

"Ruxton went back to England and Garrard returned to Cincinnati. Ruxton described his Rocky Mountain travels in a book. It is so judgmental and holier-than-thou, until he gets to the Rockies from Mexico. But in the Rockies something happened to Ruxton. He went through a kind of metamorphosis and lost his snobbishness. After living with the trappers that winter, he no longer regarded other people as less than himself. The Rockies made him human. He came away from Pikes Peak a different man; he brought with him the mountain man's lifestyle and language and preserved them forever in his books. But he left his heart there.

"As for Garrard, after he wrote his book about his experiences, *Wah-to-Yah and the Taos Trail,* he dropped from sight. However, he met Ruxton again in Buffalo, New York, of all places. Ruxton was on his way back to the Rockies, but he never made it. He died of dysentery in St. Louis in 1848, just short of his goal. And so ends the chapter on Ruxton and Garrard."

"And Gabe Wiggins?"asked Paul, relighting his pipe.

"Ah, yes," I replied, "Gabe Wiggins. Well, you know most of the particulars. Maybe you should tell me."

Paul reflected for a moment, puffing his pipe and raising his face to the stars. "Well, I'll tell you what I think. First off, I don't think he headed to California with Kearny. It doesn't fit that a commander would have a suspected killer involved in a big operation on the coast. There's no way, as I see it. Just no way. Did he go back to Bent's Fort? I don't think so. That would have been as bad as staying in Santa Fe — a real scary alternative. Did he head into the desert? No, again. He didn't know that countryside; besides, most of it's a wasteland. So, what does that leave? The mountains! A sanctuary. Perhaps right here! Yes, that would work."

"Why?"

"For one thing, he knew the trapper types from Bent's Fort. He grew up with them, right? For another thing, he knew about Taos; that it was part of the Bent's Fort operation; that St. Vrain and Charles Bent were here — they were, weren't they?"

"Yes."

"O.K. Taos and the Taos mountains are a perfect compromise between home and Santa Fe. Besides, from here he could keep an eye on that woman in Santa Fe. So, Gabe Wiggins flees Santa Fe, heads up into the hills, vanishes among the mountain men, takes up a new identity perhaps, and lives here till it's safe to go back home.When that time comes, he rides down from the mountains, settles on some land and starts a ranch. He marries, has kids, and so on."

"Would you stay up here for twenty years?"

"Hell, yes! Especially if I thought I'd killed someone."

As the fire dwindled, I realized that I would never know the whole truth about Gabe Wiggins. He would end up like others who simply slip into anonymity. But down deep I felt that Paul was right

— Gabe had made it to Taos, or near Taos, and lived as a fugitive in these hills. It all fit, fit elegantly. I did, however, think of a last-ditch possibility to find out more information.

Before we turned in I said to Paul, "You don't mind stopping in Trinidad on the way back, do you? I'd like to say hi to Cal and Barbara and see if there's something else Barbara could tell me."

The next morning we gathered our things and started on the road back to Taos. To our right, the Rio Grande valley flashed between the trees, and the gold sliver of water sparkled in the gray-green meadows below the mesas. The sun, still frail, fell harmlessly on our shoulders.

There are some lines of Swinburne that I have always liked, and I remembered them now:

> . . . That no life lives forever;
> That dead men rise up never;
> That even the weariest river
> Winds somewhere safe to sea.

Below us the Rio Grande flowed ceaselessly, fed by myriad streams, creeks, springs, and brooks, like anonymous lives sustaining the mainstream. For Gabe Wiggins, for them all, their famous, not-so-famous, and brief lives poured forth, merged, changed color and texture, and forever altered and invigorated the sweeping current of their times. And still the river flowed, gorged with new life.

Paul turned to me and said, "Say, I could get used to this walking. Maybe we should keep on going — all the way to the state border!"

"Paul, you're nuts!" I protested. "Besides, I was looking forward to riding back in that red bucket of bolts."

"Bucket of bolts! Hey, keep your voice down! You might hurt its feelin's."

"Just kidding. C'mon, let's get back to Colorado."

And so we did. The road pulled us down between cedar forest and dandelion meadow, between the proud, hulking mountains on one side and the distant, pale New Mexican buttes on the other, pulled us down toward the bright river and home.

References

De Voto, Bernard. *The Year of Decision, 1846.* Boston: Houghton Mifflin Co., 1943.

Dickey, Roland F. *New Mexico Village Arts.* Albuquerque: University of New Mexico Press, 1949.

Doughty, Howard. *Francis Parkman.* New York: Macmillan and Company, 1962.

Garrard, Lewis H. *Wah-to-Yah and the Taos Trail.* Norman: University of Oklahoma Press, 1955.

Gregg, Josiah. *Commerce of the Prairies.* Norman: University of Oklahoma Press, 1947.

Gregg, Josiah. *Diary and Letters of Josiah Gregg.* Norman: University of Oklahoma Press, 1941.

Horgan, Paul. *Great River: The Rio Grande in North American History.* Vol. 2. New York: Rinehart and Company, 1954.

Irving, Washington. *Tour on the Prairies.* Norman: University of Oklahoma Press, 1952.

Lavender, David. *Bent's Fort.* New York: Doubleday and Company, 1954.

Magoffin, Susan Shelby. *Down the Santa Fe Trail and into Mexico.* New Haven: Yale University Press, 1926.

Mails, Thomas E. *The Pueblo Children of the Earth Mother.* New York: Doubleday and Company, 1983.

Parkman, Francis. *The Oregon Trail.* New York: New American Library, 1950 edition.

Ruxton, George Frederick. *Life in the Far West.* Norman: University of Oklahoma Press, 1951.

Sprague, Marshall. *The Great Gates.* Boston: Little, Brown and Company, 1964.

Wade, Mason, ed. *The Journals of Francis Parkman.* New York: Harper and Brothers, 1947.

Wiggins, Gabriel. Journal. Unpublished.